States of Global Insecurity

Policy, Politics, and Society

Contemporary Social Issues

George Ritzer, *Series Editor*

Contemporary Social Issues

Series Editor: George Ritzer, *University of Maryland*

States of Global Insecurity

Policy, Politics, and Society

Daniel Béland

University of Calgary

Worth Publishers

Publisher: Catherine Woods
Acquisitions Editor: Sarah Berger
Marketing Manager: Amy Shefferd
Photo Editor: Patricia Marx
Art Director: Barbara Reingold
Senior Designer, Cover Designer: Kevin Kall
Associate Managing Editor: Tracey Kuehn
Project Editors: Dana Kasowitz
          Julie Smith, Matrix Publishing Services
Production Manager: Barbara Anne Seixas
Composition: Matrix Publishing Services
Printing and Binding: RR Donnelley

ISBN-13: 978-0-7167-7187-6
ISBN-10: 0-7167-7187-X

Worth Publishers
41 Madison Avenue
New York, NY 10010
www.worthpublishers.com

I dedicate this book to my wife Angela, a wonderful Texan who read this manuscript more than once. I love her and hope we will never live in fear.

About the Author

D aniel Béland is Associate Professor of Sociology at the University of Calgary. A political sociologist analyzing politics and public policy from a comparative and historical perspective, his published works include *Social Security: History and Politics from the New Deal to the Privatization Debate* and more than thirty scholarly articles. His current research addresses issues ranging from nationalism and social policy to globalization and the role of ideas in politics. You can find out more about Professor Béland's work on his Web site: www.danielbeland.org

Contents

Foreword

In the early twenty-first century, we confront a seemingly endless array of pressing social issues: war, AIDS, global warming, global and national inequality, unequal healthcare, urban decay, rampant consumerism, national and personal debt, and many more. Although such problems are regularly dealt with in newspapers, magazines, and trade books and on radio, television and the Internet, such popular treatments have severe limitations. By examining these issues systematically through the lens of sociology, we can gain greater insight into, and be better able to deal with, them. It is to this end that that this series on contemporary social issues is devoted.

Each book in the series casts a new and distinctive light on a familiar social issue, while challenging the conventional view, which may obscure as much as it clarifies. Phenomena that seem disparate and unrelated are shown to have many commonalities and to reflect a major, but often unrecognized, trend within the larger society. Or a systematic comparative investigation demonstrates the existence of social causes or consequences that are overlooked by other types of analysis. In uncovering such realities the books in this series are much more than intellectual exercises; they have powerful practical implications for our lives and for the structure of society.

At another level, this series fills a void in book publishing. There is certainly no shortage of academic titles, but those books tend to be introductory texts for undergraduates or advanced monographs for professional scholars. Missing are broadly accessible, issue-oriented books appropriate for all students (and for general readers). The books in this series occupy that niche somewhere between popular trade books and monographs. Like trade books, they deal with important and interesting social issues, are well written, and are as jargon free as possible. However, they are more rigorous than trade books in meeting academic standards for writing and research. Although they are not textbooks, they often explore topics covered in basic textbooks and therefore are easily integrated into the curriculum of sociology and other disciplines.

Each of the books in the "Contemporary Social Issues" series is a new and distinctive piece of work. I believe that students, serious general readers, and professors will all find the books to be informative, interesting, thought-provoking, and exciting.

—*George Ritzer*

Preface

We all remember September 11, 2001. For me, that was my first teaching day as a tenure-track faculty member. I was nervous about the beginning of classes and did not go online or watch television before leaving home. When I arrived at school, I saw students watching large TV screens that were unusually displayed in a corridor. I asked a student, "What's going on?" After she told me that a plane had crashed in New York City, I did not take the time to listen to the story at that moment: I had my first lecture to teach in barely forty-five minutes!

Just as I arrived at my office, Angela, who later became my wife, called me. "I'm all right," she said. I didn't understand what was going on. In 2001, she was living and working in downtown Washington, DC, where we had met two years earlier. And then she told me the whole story: two planes had crashed on the World Trade Center, which later collapsed; another plane had hit the Pentagon; another plane had crashed in Pennsylvania. This was stunning news to me, and I discussed this enormous event with my students during my first lecture. Who did it? What would happen next? What could be the long-term consequences of the attacks?

Fortunately, a new wave of terrorist attacks on the United States, which many anticipated in the days following September 11, did not materialize. Still, more than 3,000 people lost their lives that day in what remain the largest and most spectacular terrorist attacks of all time. This is why we cannot forget that day, which has become the symbol of global insecurity for many of us. But global insecurity does not only take the form of terrorism and violence. From unemployment to environmental disasters, collective insecurity takes many different forms. This book is about how state and political leaders deal with collective insecurity at the era of globalization.

Three major events of 2005 illustrate the multiple faces of collective insecurity: the London subway bombings, the New Orleans disaster, and, finally, the spectacular riots that set ablaze France's deprived suburbs. Though these events seem to have little in common, the debates on them share a few striking features. First, in all of these cases, political actors faced potential blame for not taking appropriate measures to protect the population. Second, these actors attempted to shape the dominant perception of the threats themselves and the state responses to them. Finally, the three events triggered a reevaluation of existing policies dealing with these threats. Such events, as well as the four cases analyzed in this book, show that political actors make great efforts to deal with collective insecurity through their discourse and actions.

These examples suggest that, although September 11 represents the starting point of *States of Global Insecurity,* this is not just another book dealing exclusively with global terrorism and the Bush Administration. What I had in mind when I began this project was to tell informed citizens and students of politics and social problems about the diversity and the political meaning of the major collective threats we face. The only way I could do that was to bridge several policy areas that are rarely studied together in the social science literature, including the environment, criminal justice, and social policy. This endeavor to think beyond one policy area has one main goal: providing the "big picture" about the politics of insecurity and state protection, showing how political sociology can say something meaningful about some of the greatest social and political challenges of our time and the manner in which state actors respond to them.

Even though I am a specialist of American politics, I am also a student of comparative and historical sociology, which I feel is essential to understanding our world. This concise book does not provide detailed empirical data about complex policy issues, but instead offers keys for the political and sociological comprehension of collective insecurity. From this perspective, this book suggests that global insecurity is the inescapable *political* horizon of contemporary societies.

I wrote the first draft of this book while on sabbatical leave at the Kennedy School of Government (Harvard University). Many thanks to Andrew Martin and Cathie Jo Martin for letting me present the first draft of this project at their workshop of the Center for European Studies.

I also extend my appreciation to colleagues and students who read the full manuscript: Ariel Ducey, Erin Gibbs van Brunschot, Andrew Gilchrist, Richard Podkolinski, Abdolali Rezeai, Kathryn Schneider, and Colin Wiseman. To this list, I must add Sean Hier, William Leiss, and an anonymous reader, who kindly reviewed the manuscript for Worth Publishers. I am grateful to them and to the individuals who commented upon particular chapters: François Vergniolle de Chantal (Chapter One), Martin Smith (Chapter Five), David Primo and Kathleen Sweet (Chapter Six), Simon Corley and Alice Sedar (Chapter Seven) and, finally, Edward D. Berkowitz and Mary Ruggie (Chapter Eight). Special thanks to Pierre Rosanvallon, Bruno Théret, and Charles Tilly, who provided insightful comments on the first paper I wrote on state protection. Finally, I express my deepest gratitude to the dynamic editorial team at Worth Publishers, Sarah Berger and Erik Gilg, as well as George Ritzer, who offered to publish this book in his series in the first place. I greatly benefited from their comments and encouragement.

States of Global Insecurity

Policy, Politics, and Society

Introduction

On the morning of September 11, 2001, televisions across the United States played unforgettable, tragic images of destruction. The same images that shocked the world that morning have become enduring cultural and political symbols, entering partisan discourse and greatly influencing public policy.

The September 11 attacks were political gestures that triggered debates about effective methods of fighting terrorism and the global insecurity it generates. The state is perceived now more than ever as the main source of security and protection. Nevertheless, many consider excessive state power a menace to individual rights and freedoms, and the preservation of comprehensive legal and constitutional limitations to state power is a necessary safeguard in democratic societies. The debate concerning the desirable scope and limits of security enforcement shows the enduring ambiguity of state protection and the fears related to excessive concentration of state power.

Furthermore, the ongoing debate over the "War on Terror" shows the crucial role of political leaders in the construction of threats that justify state protection. During the 2004 United States presidential campaign, for example, the Republican Party ran a television advertisement featuring menacing wolves roaming a dark forest. After stating that "John Kerry and the liberals in Congress voted to slash America's intelligence operations," the ad warned viewers that "Weakness attracts those who are waiting to do America harm."[1] In a campaign centered on issues of terrorism and national security, the Republican message was clear: only George W. Bush and the Republican Party could protect the United States against predatory terrorists. Only a few weeks before the ad appeared on television, sociologist Robb Willer published an article demonstrating that insecurity related to terrorism had boosted the popularity of President Bush; between mid-September 2001 and May 2004, the issuance of terror warnings consistently increased public support for the president.[2] As this correlation demonstrates, insecurity, electoral politics, and state protection are closely linked. Debates on these issues divide citizens, policymakers, and interest groups.

State protection ranges from policing and national security to environmental protection and social policy. Maintaining a global perspective about state protection and collective insecurity is essential for understanding current debates on how to fight global terrorism, environmental disasters, and economic insecurity. *States of Global Insecurity* provides a global perspective by exploring the enduring and increasing reliance on state protection and by stressing the tradeoffs associated with the measures enacted to protect us.

This global perspective leads to a comparative analysis of the politics of insecurity related to the development of state protection. Throughout this book, the term "politics of insecurity" refers to the ways in which political actors deal with a growing number of collective threats. Because this affects how state protection develops over time, I offer a broad analysis of the politics of insecurity taking place in four policy arenas that illustrate the multiple faces of state protection in advanced industrial societies:[3] food safety, aviation security, policing, and healthcare. These four areas of state protection involve recurring processes through which political leaders participate in the construction of collective insecurity. Each case study will show how leaders shape the way citizens perceive collective threats like economic insecurity, environmental disasters, and global terrorism.

The two main concepts featured in this book are collective insecurity and state protection. Insecurity refers both to a subjective feeling of anxiety and to a concrete lack of protection.[4] *Collective* insecurity emphasizes the social construction of these two components.[5]

For sociologists, social construction means that social and political actors collectively make sense of the world.[6] From this perspective, collective insecurity emerges when a threat is widely defined as a social and political issue.[7] Such collective insecurity is "the product of processes by which groups and individuals learn to acquire or create *interpretations of risk*. These interpretations provide rules of how to select, order, and explain signals emanating from the environment."[8] Once sources of insecurity, such as global warming, unemployment, and terrorism, are defined as collective problems that could hurt many citizens, they enter the policy agenda. The following analysis of the politics of insecurity stresses how political leaders address forms of collective insecurity.

Any sociological analysis of collective insecurity must consider the concrete nature of the threats at stake. The politics of insecurity is grounded in a "threat infrastructure;" perceived threats create specific constraints and opportunities for the political leaders who deal with them.[9] For example, episodic and spectacular threats like terrorist attacks cause greater and more sudden waves of collective anxiety than more structural and less dramatic sources of insecurity, such as the lack of healthcare coverage.

What is state protection? To answer this question, we must place it in the context of modern state building. Throughout this book, the word "state" is used in the European sense: a set of institutions at the center of a geographically bounded territory that has the power to make and enforce the rules that govern civil society, that is, the social world as it is distinct from state institutions.[10] The modern state fulfills four main tasks: first, *protecting* citizens against internal and external threats while guaranteeing formal rights; second, *regulating* the economic and social life through public education, lawmaking, and monetary policy; third, *redistributing* material and symbolic resources; and fourth, *extracting* fiscal resources to finance the first three tasks.

The first of these tasks, state protection, refers to policy interventions that fight collective insecurity through the reduction of economic, environmental, and security threats.[11] The distinction between state protection and the three other tasks is porous; in many contexts the four tasks of the modern state are related. For example, economic regulation is frequently linked to income redistribution and the protection of social rights through the welfare state.

Social and political mobilization affects these four types of state intervention. Partly because of that, these tasks change over time and from place to place. Moreover, the development of new state programs that perform these four tasks creates enduring vested interests, as people who benefit from these programs seek to preserve them. For example, once the state begins a program to distribute financial benefits to the elderly population, as with American Social Security, implementing cutbacks or dismantling the program becomes increasingly difficult; beneficiaries organize politically to defend state protection against economic insecurity.[12]

States of Global Insecurity does not argue that people are "afraid of the wrong things." This phrase, borrowed from the subtitle of Barry Glassner's 1999 book, *The Culture of Fear: Why Americans Are Afraid of the Wrong Things,*[13] featured in Michael Moore's controversial 2002 movie, *Bowling for Columbine*, indicates the belief that media outlets distract people from "serious" social and economic problems by making a fuss about spectacular yet statistically rare events like high school shootings, road rage, and workplace violence.[14] From this perspective, such media reports participate in a "culture of fear" that instills irrational and unfounded paranoia in its citizens.[15] *States of Global Insecurity* is not a moralistic attempt to denounce what some observers depict as irrational beliefs.[16] The discussion here focuses on the relationship between politics, collective insecurity, and the public policies that are meant to protect citizens; and, though it acknowledges that certain threats are blown out of proportion or even fabricated, it takes a detached look at state protection and the politics of insecurity.

More important, this book is not mainly about repressive use of fear and insecurity. Though repressive fear *may* become a tool of domination, as it was during the era of McCarthyism,[17] focusing exclusively on this repression obscures the positive role of the state in the reduction of collective insecurity. It is misleading to depict fear as the product of political machinations without acknowledging that the state can effectively reduce fear and insecurity through the implementation of policies like social programs.

As the title suggests, *States of Global Insecurity* is not about the United States only. The goal of this book is to formulate a comparative, historical perspective on collective insecurity and the ways in which political leaders deal with it. To understand better the far-reaching political ideas that shape our world, we must look beyond the United States and beyond our own era, into the history of the modern state.

States of Global Insecurity articulates two sets of arguments. First, state protection is increasingly complex and multifaceted. Globalization complicates the role of the state and can make citizens feel less secure; although globalization does not lead to a rapid decline of the state, it can affect both state protection and the politics of insecurity surrounding it.

Second, collective insecurity and state protection are largely shaped by political forces. While the mass media plays a significant role, political leaders are directly involved in the construction of the threats against which the state protects its citizens. The framing of such threats is related to electoral strategies and existing vested interests. Still, while political leaders can influence the perception of particular threats, the forms of collective insecurity they address are usually grounded in concrete economic, social, or environmental trends; consequently, the capacity of these leaders to shape public perceptions is not unlimited.

This book has two parts. Adopting a broad perspective on state making and collective insecurity, Part I offers insight on the development of state protection, paving the way to the subsequent, detailed analysis of the politics of insecurity. Part II takes a closer look at the construction of collective insecurity. After sketching a framework for the analysis of the politics of insecurity, this part explores four case studies: the British BSE ("Mad Cow Disease") episode of the mid-1990s, the transformation of aviation security in the United States before and after the events of September 11, 2001, the debate over crime and delinquency at the center of the 2002 French presidential campaign, and the contemporary American debate over health insurance coverage. These four cases are recent, widely debated, and well documented, and they illustrate the multiple faces of modern state protection.

Notes

1. Associated Press (2004), "Bush Ad Uses Wolves to Imply Kerry Weak: Democrats Counter with Eagle-Ostrich Spot," MSNBC News, October 22 (available online at www.msnbc.msn.com/id/6308153/ [accessed March 2007]).
2. Willer (2004), "The Effects of Government-Issued Terror Warnings on Presidential Approval Ratings," *Current Research in Social Psychology* 10 (1), September (available online at www.uiowa.edu/%7Egrpproc/crisp/crisp10_1.pdf [accessed March 2007]).
3. Throughout this book, the term "advanced industrial societies" refers mainly to contemporary North American and Western European countries.
4. For a discussion on the meaning of insecurity, see Lars Orsberg (1998), *Economic Insecurity*, SPRC Discussion Paper 88 (Sydney, Australia: Social Policy Research Centre, University of New South Wales).
5. Fear and anxiety do not have exactly the same meaning; fear refers to "an immediate response to risk or danger" and anxiety points to "a generalized non-immediate apprehension." See Alan Hunt, "Anxiety and Social Explanation: Some Anxieties about Anxieties," *Journal of Social History* 32(3), 509–529.
6. On the idea that the world is socially constructed, see Peter Berger and Thomas Luckmann (1967), *The Social Construction of Reality: A Treatise in the Sociology of Knowledge* (New York: Anchor Books).

   For discussion on the social construction of insecurity centered on national security, see Anthony D. Lott, (2004), *Creating Insecurity: Realism, Constructivism, and US Security Policy* (London: Ashgate); and Jutta Weldes et al. (1999), *Cultures of Insecurity: States, Communities, and the Production of Danger* (Minneapolis: University of Minnesota Press).

   On the social construction of insecurity, see also Mary Douglas and Aaron Wildavsky, *Risk and Culture* (Berkeley: University of California Press); and Mary Douglas (1992), *Risk and Blame: Essays in Cultural Theory* (London: Routledge).

   On the debate over constructivism in risk analysis, see Peter Taylor-Gooby and Jens O. Zinn (2006), "Current Directions in Risk Analysis Research: New Developments in Psychology and Sociology," *Risk Analysis* 26(2): 397–411.

7. To an extent, this is what Wright Mills labeled "sociological imagination;" see C. Wright Mills (1959), *The Sociological Imagination* (New York: Oxford University Press).

8. Jeanne X. Kasperson, Roger E. Kasperson, Nick Pidgeon, and Paul Slovic (2003), "The Social Amplification of Risk: Assessing Fifteen Years of Research and Theory" in Nick Pidgeon, Roger E. Kasperson, and Paul Slovic, eds., *The Social Amplification of Risk* (Cambridge: Cambridge University Press), pp. 13–46.

9. The concept of a threat infrastructure refers to the concrete risks specific to a policy area. For more on this concept, see Chapter Two.

   For a discussion on the *political* differences between particular threats, see Thomas A. Birkland (1997), *After Disaster: Agenda Setting, Public Policy, and Focusing Events* (Washington, DC: Georgetown University Press).

10. John A. Hall and John Ikenberry (1989), *The State* (Minneapolis: University of Minnesota Press), pp. 1–2. In the United States, this set of institutions is generally referred to as "government."

11. Alexis de Tocqueville was one of the first modern authors to examine the concept of state protection (*l'État-protecteur*). See Tocqueville (1840, rpt. 2000), *Democracy in America* (Chicago: University of Chicago Press); see also Pierre Rosanvallon (1990), *L'État en France de 1789 à nos jours* (Paris: Le Seuil).

12. See Daniel Béland (2007), *History and Politics from the New Deal to the Privatization Debate*, Paperback Edition with New Afterword (Lawrence: University Press of Kansas); Andrea Louise Campbell (2003), *How Policies Make Citizens: Senior Citizen Activism and the American Welfare State* (Princeton: Princeton University Press); and Paul Pierson (1994), *Dismantling the Welfare State? Reagan, Thatcher, and the Politics of Retrenchment* (Cambridge: Cambridge University Press).

13. *The Culture of Fear: Why Americans Are Afraid of the Wrong Things* (New York: Basic Books). For a critique of Glassner's book, see Andrew Tudor (2003), "A (Macro) Sociology of Fear?" *The Sociological Review* 51(2): 218–237.

   In a recent book, Peter N. Stearns adopts a historical perspective on the "culture of fear" that allegedly characterizes the United States: Stearns (2006), *American Fear* (New York: Routledge).

14. For a systematic analysis of the relationship between fear and media reports, see David L. Altheide (2002), *Creating Fear: News and the Construction of Crisis* (New York: Aldine de Gruyter).

   For an analysis that concentrates on media accounts and the role of political actors in the construction of a particular threat, see David L. Altheide (2006), *Terrorism and the Politics of Fear* (Lanham: AltaMira).

15. Frank Furedi (2002), *Culture of Fear: Risk-Taking and the Morality of Low Expectations*, Second Edition (London: Continuum Books). For a critique of Furedi's "panic about those who panic," see Tony Fitzpatrick (2005), *New Theories of Welfare* (Houndmills: Palgrave), p. 81.
16. For a critique of this approach, see Lee Clarke (2006), *Worst Cases: Terror and Catastrophe in the Popular Imagination* (Chicago: University of Chicago Press), pp. 35–41.
17. Corey Robin (2004), *Fear: The History of a Political Idea* (Oxford: Oxford University Press). "McCarthyism" refers to rampant radical anti-communism in the United States from the late-1940s to the mid-1950s.

PART I

Mapping State Protection

Introduction to Part I

Providing the necessary historical background to the comparative analysis of the politics of insecurity featured in Part II, the following chapters clarify major theoretical claims about state protection while mapping its development from policing and national security to social policy and protection against environmental hazards.

Three chapters comprise Part I. Chapter One discusses four major claims about the development of modern state protection that will guide the book's analysis. Chapter Two explores the multifaceted and increasingly complex nature of state protection by exploring the characteristics and the "threat infrastructure" of the four policy areas featured in the case studies of Part II. Chapter Three features a broad discussion about the possible impact of globalization on state protection and the politics of insecurity.

What Is State Protection?

In industrial societies since the nineteenth century, broad economic, social, and political transformations have led to the expansion of state protection. The modern state is now a major source of economic and physical security; citizens rely on the state for everything from environmental policy to national security to transportation safety. Boundaries of state protection remain contested, intensifying traditional debates about liberty, personal responsibility, and the proper allocation of fiscal resources. How far should the state go to protect its citizens?

The three sections of this chapter make four claims about the nature and development of state protection. The first section uses sociologist Charles Tilly's seminal 1985 work on state making, "War Making and State Making as Organized Crime," as a starting point for the study of state protection and the politics of insecurity. This section claims that political leaders may help create the threats against which they claim to protect the population.

The next section emphasizes the claim that state protection extends beyond the policing and national security that are so central to Tilly's work. Though they do not form a coherent set of institutions, the multiple faces of state protection increase citizens' reliance on the modern state. To illustrate the complex nature of state protection in advanced industrial societies, this section presents the examples of social policy and the expansion of risk management policy since the nineteenth century.

The third section claims that it is impossible to understand major forms of state protection without looking at their interactions with alternative providers of protection, discussing the changing relationship between the state and these alternative providers in modern societies. This section also introduces the final claim that, as with any other form of state intervention, fighting collective threats involves inherently political fiscal and moral tradeoffs.

14

State Making as "Organized Crime"

Like the feudal system it slowly replaced, the modern state was largely the product of military conquests that fueled physical insecurity throughout Europe. Before the advent of the modern state in Western Europe, extended family and the feudal system were the main providers of economic and physical protection.[1] The feudal system was ostensibly mutually advantageous to both landowners and their tenants: vassals pledged "oaths of fealty" to their masters, vowing to work in exchange for land and military support. Feudalism thus grounded protection in personal obligation.[2]

Charles Tilly's provocative paper "War Making and State Making as Organized Crime" stresses the ambiguous nature of modern state protection in a discussion of state building in feudal and early modern Europe.[3] Tilly identifies the broad political logic, still at play in our modern world, that war making and state making are closely related. Furthermore, Tilly presents an analogy between these two processes and "organized crime. . . . Banditry, piracy, gangland rivalry, policing, and war making belong to the same continuum."[4] To support this analogy, Tilly defines "protection:"

> In contemporary American parlance, the word "protection" sounds two contrasting tones. One is comforting, the other ominous. With one tone, "protection" calls up images of the shelter against danger provided by a powerful friend, a large insurance policy, or a sturdy roof. With the other, it evokes the racket in which a local strong man forces merchants to pay tribute in order to avoid damage—damage the strong man himself threatens to deliver.[5]

The early development of the modern state is thus analogous to extortion, as state actors often dramatize or even fabricate violent threats in order to justify their existence and reinforce their power.[6]

Without going as far as reducing emerging state power to pure violence, Tilly recognizes the centrality of force and war making in the process of state building and the development of state protection in largely Western Europe. In medieval and early modern Europe, state making was the product of conquests and the elimination of local rivals, military expansion that depended on "the business of selling protection . . . whether people want it or not."[7] Likewise, the modern state depends on a process whereby populations pay fiscal (taxes) and human (military service) prices for protection they would not necessarily seek independently.

Over the long run, agents of the state create stable, relatively centralized organizations that shape the modern state's sovereignty. According to Tilly, they do so through four different activities: war making (eliminating external rivals), state making (eliminating internal rivals or dissidents), protection (eliminating the enemies of clients), and extraction (acquiring the means to pursue the three other activities). These activities take different forms, but all "depend on the state's tendency to monopolize the concentrated means of coercion"[8] —once in place, the state gradually eliminates or absorbs competing forms of protection and fiscal extraction.[9]

Though popular resistance can lead to concessions from the state, such as guarantees of rights and representative institutions, the modern state is still the product of violent conquest and imposed protection and extraction. Indeed, before the twentieth century, "any state that failed to put considerable effort in war making was likely to disappear."[10] Without sustained war-making efforts, especially the creation of a national army financed through a centralized taxation system, state making cannot lead to the establishment of a lasting political and territorial order. In this context, protecting the population against threats of violence is the best justification for taxation.

Tilly's analysis stresses that state actors have the power to construct the threats against which they claim to protect the population. President George W. Bush's recent discourse on the "Axis of Evil," comprising Iraq, Iran, and North Korea, exemplifies Tilly's idea that state officials can amplify and exploit potential collective threats in order to promote their interests at home and abroad. From this perspective, the president overdramatized the international situation by depicting these countries as immediate menaces to the United States and the rest of the world.[11] The justification for the 2003 invasion of Iraq, which consisted of misleading rhetoric about Iraqi "weapons of mass destruction" and the supposed link between al Qaeda and the Hussein regime, further illustrates Tilly's point.[12]

This is not to say that the state only deals with fabricated threats. Part II of this book discusses four cases involving genuine threats to the state that favor the emergence of popular demand for protection. As will be shown, in contemporary societies, most state interventions are not imposed on society against the will of the majority; on the contrary, popular demand and interest group mobilization have long favored the development of state protection.

The Multiple Faces of State Protection

Over the last two centuries, state protection has expanded far beyond issues of policing and national security. As a result, state protection has become increasingly multifaceted. The emergence of modern social programs illustrates the growing complexity of state protection, which is further discussed in Chapter Two. Social programs protect individuals against poverty stemming from old age, unemployment, or high medical costs, and help to reduce social inequality. As T. H. Marshall wrote, as a result of these programs

> [t]here is a general enrichment of the concrete substance of civilized life, a general reduction of risk and insecurity, an equalization between the more and the less fortunate at all levels—between the healthy and the sick, the employed and the unemployed, the old and the active, the bachelor and the father of a large family.[13]

But the emergence of the modern welfare state does not necessarily lead to egalitarian fiscal redistribution between the rich and the poor. In countries like France, for example, specific occupational groups such as civil servants and employees of public enterprises enjoy a greater level of state-granted social protection than most other workers and citizens.[14]

Though they seldom provide equal protection to citizens, social insurance programs like unemployment insurance, Medicare, and Social Security protect major segments of the population against poverty and economic insecurity. Workers are formally protected against blatant exploitation and extreme deprivation through new labor codes and social programs.

The modern welfare state reflects the development of a major form of protection against economic insecurity that favors the expansion of state intervention.[15] This protection frequently takes the shape of state-granted individual rights. Joining the old liberal form of economic security based on personal savings and private ownership, a new type of rights-based security associated with the welfare state took shape during the twentieth century.[16]

As the state has provided more social programs, the doctrine of self-reliance has weakened. Prior to the inception of these programs, individuals and families, not the state, were expected to insure themselves against disability, financial loss, illness, and old age through personal savings and private insurance. Charity appeared only as a last resort, available exclusively to the poor. Modern state protection depends on the concepts that the state is at least partially responsible for the well being of its citizens and that self-reliance is inadequate against the many sources of collective insecurity. Thus, modern state protection redefines boundaries between personal and state responsibilities.

These boundaries remain contested and are the source of debates on issues ranging from welfare reform to environmental regulation and transportation safety. Who is responsible for these issues? How much should the state do to reduce forms of insecurity that some citizens may attribute to poor character and personal judgment? The massive development of state protection over the past century has not eliminated these inherently political questions, especially in the United States, where personal responsibility remains a major concern when discussing issues like welfare reform.[17]

One way to understand the expansion of state protection is to examine the growing role of the state as risk manager. In the United States, for example, risk management policy, "any governmental activity designed either to reduce or to reallocate risks,"[18] passed through three major historical phases. In the first phase, the state provided security for business (to 1900); in the second, security for workers (1900–1960); and in the third, security for all (since the 1960s).[19]

In the first phase, risk management was used as an instrument of economic growth. Nineteenth-century risk-management measures on banking, bankruptcy, and limited liability protected investors and businesspeople against economic risks.[20] The state increasingly acted as a risk manager to stimulate the expansion of capitalism, becoming a crucial component of the capitalist economy.

The second phase corresponds to the welfare state moment itself, with the advent of social insurance.[21] As opposed to social assistance, social insurance is seldom genuinely redistributive. Through the compulsory contributions of payroll taxes, the state forces workers to subscribe to social insurance plans that protect them against economic insecurity.[22] In addition to providing social insurance, the state attempts to reduce the number of work-related accidents through workplace safety legislation. At first designed to protect targeted groups such as women and children, this protective legislation has since been extended to the entire working population.[23]

The third phase spread risk management policy to the protection of all citizens against economic insecurity.[24] From disaster relief to product liability, modern risk management policies protect residents and consumers, not only businesspeople and workers. The policies generated by this phase are the thorniest in issues of protection versus personal responsibility, particularly in matters of product liability. During the nineteenth century, liability laws favored producers over consumers, who could seldom recover losses from a seller after buying a defective product. At the time, producers could not be held responsible for defective merchandise, thus consumers were not protected against negligent manufacturers. In the 1960s, the state, through several court decisions, began to protect consumers by making manufacturers liable for faulty or dangerous products: "As successful product liability suits became more and more common, manufacturers discovered that the doctrine of *caveat emptor* had been completely inverted. Now sellers, rather than buyers, had to 'beware' every time a good was sold."[25]

Insurance guarantee funds represent another method through which the state shields citizens against the negative consequences of private markets. In recent decades, most American states have established insurance guarantee funds that protect consumers against the insolvency (lack of financial resources) of private insurance companies. These funds return at least part of the claims from these companies to consumers who have a policy with them. Through this original form of public insurance, lawmakers once again act as "insurers of last resorts."[26] By spreading insolvency insurance risks, these funds have transformed the state into a safety net for consumers. Not formally related to social rights, insurance guarantee funds illustrate the expansion of state protection in the field of risk management.

The example of insurance guarantee funds indicates the complex relationship between private and public forms of protection.[27] In this case, public insurance reinforces private protection instead of replacing it, compensating for what is commonly described as a "market failure." In other policy areas, however, the state and private providers of protection compete.

From families and community associations to criminal organizations and private insurance companies, other actors and institutions constitute alternative sources of protection against collective insecurity. None of these alternative providers of protection can match the far-reaching power of the state. Yet the development of state protection affects these alternative providers, which can in turn affect state building. As recent studies show, the analysis of public policy must take into account alternative providers,[28] especially the private providers of protection who compete with the state for resources and legitimacy.[29] Because the business of protection is often lucrative, private providers are likely to oppose the expansion of public policies that reduce the role of the private sector. For example, the American health insurance industry has long opposed the development of national health insurance, a measure that could make their industry far less profitable. Well-established private provisions such as private health insurance are therefore likely to become an obstacle to the expansion of state protection.

A Matter of Political Choice

State protection has significant costs, monetary or otherwise, and is, as a result, the product of policy choices that involve significant tradeoffs.[30] Consequently, state officials must balance protection imperatives with other priorities and decide which forms of protection should be prioritized.[31] Arbitrating conflicting demands and values, an inherently political process, is a significant part of the politics of insecurity and state protection.

One such tradeoff is personal liberty: citizens and interest groups may oppose state initiatives because they inhibit their freedom or impose new taxes. Gun control and tobacco legislation are two such examples of contested forms of state protection that certain citizens feel are imposed on them for illegitimate reasons. But more important, state protection may jeopardize individual rights on a constitutional and moral level.

After the attacks of September 11, 2001, citizens and interest groups alike pressured elected officials to protect them more effectively against terrorism. In the weeks following the attacks, Congress enacted major legislation such as the Patriot Act. Today this measure has raised concern regarding how the state should balance national security and individual rights and freedoms.[32] The Act, signed into law by President Bush on October 26, 2001, "enhanced the executive branch's powers to conduct surveillance, search for money-laundering, share intelligence with criminal prosecutors, and charge suspected terrorists with crimes."[33] Though the Act was put into law ostensibly to neutralize potential terrorist threats, it has been widely criticized by human rights advocates.[34] Overall, the increased surveillance capacities of the state and the related development of new surveillance technologies have been denounced as a major threat to personal rights and freedoms.[35] In the years to come, the balance between civil rights and the imperative of national security will remain at the center of public debate.

Auto safety provides another example of the perceived conflict between personal freedom and state protection. When the state enacts legislation that requires car drivers and passengers to wear seatbelts, it forces them to alter their personal behavior to fit a state-imposed definition of security. Some individuals see seatbelt laws as major infringements on personal freedom. In addition, state regulations regarding vehicle safety can seriously constrain automakers in designing new car models.[36]

Laws that restrict smoking to designated areas also limit freedom and attempt to shape behavior in the name of public health, as do increased taxes on tobacco products. Should the state campaign against tobacco use and restrict the freedom of smokers because health studies suggest that secondhand smoke is a significant threat to public health?

These issues are not only moral but deeply political, involving powerful interest groups like the tobacco industry and the anti-tobacco lobby.[37] Perhaps no other issue gives us as striking an example of the power of interest group mobilization as the debate over gun control. In the United

States, the National Rifle Association annually spends millions of dollars to fight gun control initiatives in the name of personal freedom and the respect of constitutional rights.[38]

Imperatives of state protection, from national security and law enforcement to social and environmental policy, concern not only personal freedom but also the proper allocation of state resources. Tax levels are not set in stone and can increase over time, so more state intervention in one area does not necessarily mean less in another. Still, elected officials must set priorities and allocate limited resources to a growing number of programs.

Policymakers commonly think in terms of probabilities when allocating resources, because spending money on disasters that are more likely to occur seems the best approach considering the relative scarcity of fiscal resources. Experts and political leaders can prioritize threats that are more likely to materialize and cause harm to large segments of the population. On the other hand, some statistically improbable yet possible catastrophes are so frightening that they could merit state action:

> If we imagine the future in terms of probabilities, then risks look safe. That's because any future big event is unlikely. You're probably not going to die tomorrow. Terrorists probably won't destroy the White House, the Sears Tower, and Harvard University all in the same day. Four tornadoes probably won't converge on Toledo at the same time. . . . If we imagine the future in terms of possibilities, however, horrendous scenarios appear. Could there be an accidental detonation of a nuclear weapon? Yes, there could. Could a hurricane stall over Miami, slip back out the sea, then loop back into Miami again? Definitely.[39]

Though such catastrophic events may never occur, some argue that the state and citizens should be prepared for them. That said, the number of possible but statistically improbable large-scale threats is so immense that, in order to protect the populace against every contingency, the state would need to spend infinitely more on disaster prevention than it currently does. Moreover, the number of possible sources of disaster is so great that it is impossible to ensure that the extra spending would make the world a safer place. In the future, however, perhaps a greater emphasis on "worst-case" possibilities could balance out the one of probabilities, which remains dominant.[40]

Popular consensus on the most pressing issues of the day is difficult to achieve, and even once priorities and adequate spending levels have been agreed on, elected officials must decide who should bear the costs of existing and proposed protection measures. Should the state tax younger workers in order to guarantee the economic security of the elderly? Should the airline industry bear the costs of aviation safety and security? These are inherently political questions that set citizens, politicians, and interest groups in opposition. As we will discuss in subsequent chapters, even the perception of the threats that raise such questions is largely political.

Decisions of resource allocation also have an impact on social inequality; public policies do not affect all citizens uniformly, and policy design shapes protection measures for particular segments of the population. For example, potentially repressive forms of state protection (like the zero-tolerance policies discussed in the next chapter) may target the poor and/or minorities. These groups may bear the cost of measures enacted to reduce popular anxiety on crime and national security. State protection is a political issue partly because it involves a collective struggle over which a segment of society can gain from the measures put in place, but which they can also lose.

Resource allocation and the development of state protection varies greatly from one country to another, even when countries face similar threats. For example, Sweden's welfare state is much more comprehensive than that of the United States. Sweden's welfare state guarantees universal access to social services and health care, reducing poverty and income inequality. But this strong welfare state comes at a cost: Swedes pay much higher taxes on average than do Americans. To compensate for meager social benefits and services (for example, no national health insurance), however, many Americans save for retirement and pay health insurance premiums or gain health insurance coverage through their employer or spouse's employer. The role of such private forms of protection increases social inequality, as millions of citizens cannot or do not save for retirement, or pay increasingly higher health insurance premiums.[41]

Countries with similar levels of economic development thus create distinct policies and institutional arrangements to fight similar threats. In the next chapter, the nature of the threats themselves is addressed: how does the nature of each threat help to construct collective insecurity?

Notes

1. This discussion draws on Daniel Béland (2005), "Insecurity, Citizenship, and Globalization: The Multiple Faces of State Protection," in *Sociological Theory* 23(1) 2005: 25–41.
2. See Marc Bloch (1939, rpt. 1982), *Feudal Society: Social Classes and Political Organization* (Chicago: University of Chicago Press); Norbert Elias (1994), *The Civilizing Process: Sociogenetic and Psychogenetic Investigations*, Revised Edition (London: Blackwell); F. L. Ganshof (1961), *Feu-*

dalism (New York: Harper); and Joseph R. Strayer (1965), *Feudalism* (Princeton, NJ: Van Nostrand).

3. Charles Tilly (1985), "War Making and State Making as Organized Crime," in Peter B. Evans, Dietrich Rueschmeyer, and Theda Skocpol, eds., *Bringing the State Back In* (Cambridge: Cambridge University Press), pp. 169–91.

   For more general considerations concerning the emergence of the modern state, see Gianfranco Poggi (1978), *The Development of the Modern State: A Sociological Introduction* (Stanford, CA: Stanford University Press), and Joseph R. Strayer (1970), *On the Medieval Origins of the Modern State* (Princeton: Princeton University Press).

   For a discussion of modern state theories, see Louis Irving Horowitz (1999), *Behemoth: Main Currents in the History and Theory of Political Sociology* (New Brunswick, NJ: Transaction Publishers).

4. Tilly, p. 170.

5. Ibid.

6. On the analogy between state making and protection rackets, see also Vadim Volkov (2002), *Violent Entrepreneurs: The Use of Force in the Making of Russian Capitalism* (Ithaca: Cornell University Press).

7. Tilly, p. 175.

8. Ibid., p. 181.

9. For an alternative view on the emergence of the modern state that stresses the role of economic factors, see Hendrik Spruyt (1994), *The Sovereign State and Its Competitors: An Analysis of Systems Change* (Princeton: Princeton University Press).

10. Tilly, p. 184.

11. See, for example, Bush's 2002 State of the Union Address (Washington, DC: Office of the Press Secretary; available online at www.whitehouse.gov/news/releases/2002/01/20020129-11.html [accessed March 2007]).

    For an analysis of the international political and economic strategy of the Bush Administration following the events of September 11, 2001, see David Harvey (2003), *The New Imperialism* (New York, Oxford University Press).

12. Robert Dreyfuss and Jason Vest (2004), "The Lie Factory," in *Mother Jones*, January/February: 34–41 (available online at www.motherjones.com/news/feature/2004/01/12_405.html [accessed March 2007]). My thanks to Roland Simon for his insight on this issue.

13. T. H. Marshall (1964), "Citizenship and Social Class" in *Class, Citizenship and Development* (Garden City, NY: Doubleday), pp. 65–122. On the work of T. H. Marshall, see Bryan S. Turner, ed. (1993), *Citizenship and Social Theory* (London: Sage).

14. Peter Baldwin (1990), *The Politics of Social Solidarity: Class Bases of the European Welfare State, 1875–1975* (Cambridge, Cambridge University Press).

    In the United States and other countries, reliance on private benefits has led to a divide between those who have access to private pensions and insurance coverage and those who do not. See Jacob S. Hacker (2002), *The Divided Welfare State: The Battle over Public and Private Social Benefits in the United States* (Cambridge, Cambridge University Press).

15. According to François Ewald, the emergence of modern social insurance at the end of the nineteenth century is linked to the construction of social risks and the reconfiguration of personal responsibility. See Ewald (1986), *L'État-providence* (Paris: Grasset).

16. Robert Castel (2003), *From Manual Workers to Wage Laborers: Transformation of the Social Question* (New Brunswick, NJ: Transaction Publishers).

17. For a conservative example of rhetoric on personal responsibility in the United States, see Marvin Olasky (1992), *The Tragedy of American Compassion* (Washington, DC: Regnery Publishing).

18. David A. Moss (2001), *When All Else Fails: Government as the Ultimate Risk Manager* (Cambridge, MA: Harvard University Press), p. 1. This discussion of risk management draws extensively from Moss's book.

19. Ibid.

20. Ibid., pp. 53–151.

21. Ibid., pp. 152–215.

22. Several authors have criticized the idea of social insurance as a regressive way to insure, rather than challenge, inequality; see, for example, Jerry R. Cates (1983), *Insuring Inequality: Administrative Leadership in Social Security, 1935–1954* (Ann Arbor: University of Michigan Press).

23. Some national social insurance systems remain fragmented because of the mobilization of specific interest groups; see Baldwin, *The Politics of Social Solidarity*.

24. Moss, *When All Else Fails*, pp. 216–91.

25. Ibid., p. 9.

    These court decisions included *Henningsen v. Bloomfield Motors, Inc.*, 32 N.J. 358, 364–69 (1960). On these decisions, see Moss, *When All Else Fails*, pp. 238–49.

26. Ibid., p. 264.

27. Ibid.

28. Hacker, *The Divided Welfare State*.

    Gøsta Esping-Andersen explores the relationship between public and private protection in his 1990 book *The Three Worlds of Welfare*

Capitalism (Princeton: Princeton University Press). See also Esping-Andersen (1999), *Social Foundations of Postindustrial Economies* (New York: Oxford University Press).

29. The dividing line between public and private protection is fuzzy, particularly when the state contracts services to external, private sources. Tax incentives and state regulations affect the development of protection schemes from the private sector, and the state increasingly contracts services to private businesses that perform public safety and security tasks.

30. On this issue, with a focus on physical security, see Bruce Schneier (2003), *Beyond Fear: Thinking Sensibly about Security in an Uncertain World* (New York: Copernicus Books).

31. On this issue, see Erin Gibbs Van Brunschot and Leslie W. Kennedy (2007), *Risk Balance and Security* (Thousand Oaks, CA: Sage).

32. The post–September 11 security apparatus is not necessarily effective in fighting terrorism. For a critical analysis of this situation, see James Bovard (2003), *Terrorism and Tyranny: Trampling Freedom, Justice and Peace to Rid the World of Evil* (New York: Palgrave).

33. Amy Goldstein (2003), "Fierce Fight over Secrecy, Scope of Law; Amid Rights Debate, Law Cloaks Data on Its Impact," in the *Washington Post*, September 8: A1 (available online at www.washingtonpost.com/wp-dyn/content/article/2005/11/04/AR2005110401030.html [accessed March 2007]).

34. See, for example, Nat Hentoff (2003),"Vanishing Liberties: Where's the Press?" in the *Village Voice*, April 11 (available online at www.aaiusa.org/press-room/1990/mustread041103d [accessed March 2007]).

35. See Kevin D. Haggerty and Richard V. Ericson (1997), *Policing the Risk Society* (Toronto: University of Toronto Press); Haggerty and Ericson, eds. (2006), *The New Politics of Surveillance and Visibility* (Toronto: University of Toronto Press); and David Lyon (2003), *Surveillance after September 11* (Cambridge, MA: Polity).

36. On auto safety, see Jerry L. Mashaw and David L. Harfst (1990), *The Struggle for Auto Safety* (Cambridge, MA: Harvard University Press).

37. For comparative perspectives on this issue, see Eric A. Feldman and Roland Bayer (2004), *Unfiltered: Conflicts over Tobacco Policy and Public Health* (Cambridge: Harvard University Press), and Donley T. Studlar (2002), *Tobacco Control: Comparative Politics in the United States and Canada* (Peterborough, Ont.: Broadview Press).

On the American debate on this issue, see Robert L. Rabin and Stephen D. Sugarman, eds., (1993), *Smoking Policy: Law, Politics, and Culture* (New York: Oxford University Press).

38. For a balanced account of the American debate over gun control, see William Vizzard (2000), *Shots in the Dark: The Policy, Politics, and Symbolism of Gun Control* (Lanham, MD, Rowman & Littlefield).

39. Lee Clarke (2006), *Worst Cases: Terror and Catastrophe in the Popular Imagination* (Chicago: University of Chicago Press), p. 42.

40. Lee Clarke's discussion on worst-case scenarios follows the "precautionary principle" that where there are "threats of serious or irreversible damage, lack of full scientific certainty shall not be used as a reason for postponing cost-effective measures to prevent environmental degradation" (Rio Declaration on Environment and Development, June 14, 1992, 31 ILM 874, cited in Clarke, *Worst Cases*, p. 179).

For a critical discussion of the different understandings of this contested principle, see Cass R. Sunstein (2006), *Laws of Fear: Beyond the Precautionary Principle* (Cambridge: Cambridge University Press).

41. See Esping-Andersen, *The Three Worlds of Welfare Capitalism*; Hacker, *The Divided Welfare State*; and Jennifer Klein (2003), *For All These Rights: Business, Labor, and the Shaping of America's Public-Private Welfare State* (Princeton: Princeton University Press).

Four Policy Areas

Since the 1970s, new forms of state protection have expanded while older forms have faced fresh challenges. Confronting new economic and political pressures, contemporary national states have multiplied their protective interventions while struggling to eliminate public deficits. Despite fiscal concerns and growing ideological attacks against "big government," the state remains the most crucial provider of protection in advanced industrial societies.

This chapter reviews the transformation of four major faces of state protection in order to identify the "threat infrastructure" that distinguishes each of them, emphasizing how particular threats affect the politics of insecurity surrounding them. As argued, each protection area is characterized by a unique threat infrastructure that generates particular constraints and opportunities for political leaders. In other words, the concrete features of the threat at hand have a political meaning that the analysis of collective insecurity must take into account.

The four sections of this chapter provide a cross-national overview of the policy areas analyzed in Part II: environmental protection, especially food safety; transportation safety, especially in the aviation sector; policing, especially urban delinquency; and social policy, especially health insurance coverage. These policy areas exemplify the diversity and the multifaceted nature of contemporary state protection, and their development over the past decades illustrates both citizens' enduring reliance on the state and, in many cases, the resilience of existing forms of state protection.

While discussing variations in the threat infrastructure from one policy area to another, this chapter also examines how economic and technological change can become instrumental in creating the need for state protection, especially in issues of food and aviation safety.[1] Finally, as the section on social policy suggests, existing policies affect the politics of state protection and collective insecurity; when political leaders reform existing protection measures, they must take into account any strong vested interests that have been created by those measures.

Technological Change and State Protection

Environmental Protection

In advanced industrial societies, environmental risks stemming from technological change have long justified an expansion of state protection. Because addressing these risks requires expert knowledge and extensive regulatory power, the state remains the only actor in society that can deal with these risks comprehensively. But as new environmental challenges emerge, the mission of the state is increasingly complex and demanding.

Protecting citizens and nature against chemical and nuclear hazards has only recently become a major mission of the state. "In the modernization process, more and more *destructive* forces are . . . being unleashed, forces before which the human imagination stands in awe."[2] As events such as the 1986 Chernobyl nuclear disaster and the propagation of Bovine Spongiform Encephalopathy (BSE) illustrate, these new environmental risks may have global impact.[3]

Because environmental risks are increasingly complex and global in nature, it is impossible for the state to protect against every possible environmental catastrophe and health hazard.[4] There is an apparent contradiction between the increasingly global nature of environmental threats and the geographically bounded sovereignty of national states. The global nature of many environmental threats demands that national states join in preparing for and fighting such possibilities, leading in recent years to a growing number of international treaties and organizations. Still, the national state remains the crucial source of environmental protection in advanced industrial societies, enforcing regulations, providing citizens with disaster relief, and applying the guidelines imposed by international treaties.[5]

Environmental regulation is a deeply political issue. European and North American states have enacted measures to prevent environmental disasters, to react quickly when such disasters occur, and to reduce sources of pollution mainly in response to pressure from environmental groups and the general public.[6] And, as shown by the Bush Administration's 2005 push to allow drilling in Alaska's Arctic National Wildlife Refuge, powerful economic interests—in this case the energy lobby—can spur significant reduction in state-granted environmental protection.[7]

But such economic interests cannot always prevent the development of environmental protection. The example of nuclear power provides ground to this claim. A major energy source in several advanced industrial countries, nuclear power accounts for more than 75 percent of France's electricity needs. Though the United States relies on nuclear power for only 20 percent of its energy supply, it has more nuclear reactors in activity than any other country, partly because of its greater energy needs. Of the 442 nuclear reactors in operation worldwide as of June 2006, 103 were located in the United States.[8] The frightening prospect of a major nuclear disaster is a key aspect of contemporary environmental insecurity in many countries.

Two recent nuclear accidents increased concern over the safety of civilian nuclear energy. The first occurred in March 1979 at the Three Mile Island plant near Middletown, Pennsylvania. Though no one died as a consequence of this partial meltdown, Three Mile Island became a symbol of nuclear insecurity and triggered the enactment of new safety measures in nuclear power plants.[9] The second, the Chernobyl disaster of April 1986, was far more catastrophic, immediately killing more than thirty people, severely contaminating large regions of Belarus, Ukraine, and Russia, and forcing the evacuation and resettlement of more than 300,000 citizens. In the regions most affected, radiation exposure caused abnormal levels of cancer that may kill thousands in the decades to come. The Chernobyl tragedy increased awareness of the risks of nuclear energy, sparking global—and often successful—political mobilization against its use.[10] Overall, these two accidents forced policymakers in many countries to enact new safety measures for nuclear power plants.

Food safety, another major source of environmental insecurity in advanced industrial societies, bridges environmental and agricultural policy. Contemporary debates over food safety mesh traditional anxieties with more recent environmental concerns resulting from technological change.

Food poisoning and food scares have always been a significant aspect of human life: "All human beings before us questioned the contents of their plates."[11] During the feudal era, for example, rumors about hazardous foods and even dishes containing cat meat or human remains were common. Modern concerns about food have recently emerged as a consequence of the growing distance between food producers and consumers, which is itself a direct consequence of urbanization, industrialization, and the decline of family farming.[12]

An early example of these concerns emerged a century ago with the advent of the slaughterhouse system in the United States. In his 1906 novel, *The Jungle*, muckraking writer Upton Sinclair denounced the poor hygiene and working conditions prevailing in these slaughterhouses.[13] The novel triggered a debate over meat quality, quickly leading to the Meat Inspection Act in 1906, legislation that created a system of sanitation standards for slaughterhouses and meat processing facilities. That same year, Congress enacted the Pure Food and Drug Act, which led to the creation of the Food and Drug Administration (FDA). Today, the FDA is a federal organization, part of the Department of Health and Human Services, involved in food inspection and regulation.[14] Many other countries have created similar regulatory agencies to protect citizens against potentially hazardous consumables.

Growing awareness in recent decades of food threats related to biological, technological, and environmental hazards has created new dilemmas for experts, informed citizens, and policymakers. For example:

> Are milk and beef produced from animals injected with hormones safe? What about the genetically modified foods that are the products of plant biotechnology? And who should have final say on whether these products pose acceptable or unacceptable risks to human health?[15]

Environmental groups and other political forces pressure the agricultural industry to implement new measures to reduce food hazards,[16] and national states implement a growing number of regulations and inspection mechanisms to reduce risks such as BSE, *E. coli*, and *Salmonella*. When consumers fear buying food that seems unsafe, restoring trust in the food supply and industry may require the implementation of new safety measures such as additional inspection programs and the destruction of potentially infected crops or livestock.

The close relationship between state agencies and the food industry can undermine the effectiveness of food safety policy.[17] And as in other policy areas, safety measures have costs that are frequently passed on to consumers and taxpayers. Despite the need to maintain confidence in the food supply, some may argue that this cost is excessive because most possible food threats will never affect a large portion of the population.

Because food safety is related to both agriculture and the environment, several state agencies participate in its maintenance. In the United States, the FDA, the Department of Agriculture (USDA), and the Environmental Protection Agency (EPA) all deal with food safety. Scientific knowledge is crucial to guiding the actions of these agencies in a global trade environment:

Proper design and implementation of new food safety policies must be based on the best available science. This is especially important in an international context. Risk assessment and risk management approaches to define appropriate interventions to prevent contamination require state-of-the-art science to ensure that our risk reduction efforts are both effective and cost-efficient.[18]

Recognizing the cross-national nature of such risks, in December 2001 the European Union (EU) established the European Food Safety Authority (EFSA), which collaborates with the twenty-five EU member states. Following food scares in the 1990s, the EU concluded that it "needed to establish a new scientific body charged with providing independent and objective advice on food safety issues associated with the food chain."[19] EU member states still regulate food safety regulations within their own borders, but EFSA's development shows that cross-national model of environmental governance is emerging in the policy area.[20]

The threat infrastructure of this policy area has a number of outstanding characteristics. Because widespread incidents affecting the food supply are infrequent, food safety rarely becomes a high-profile issue. Food hazards are episodic in nature, but food safety concerns all citizens. Food hazards can affect large segments of the population, but people can change dietary habits to avoid risky food; for example, someone afraid of eating beef because of BSE can turn to other types of meat or even become vegetarian.

An increase in food insecurity may have negative consequences for the food industry. As we will discuss in Chapter Four, food safety is an issue at the center of growing risk awareness in advanced industrial societies. Food hazards are by nature invisible threats, difficult to detect and time-consuming to trace.[21]

Transportation Safety

Like environmental protection, transportation safety is directly related to technological change. Since the nineteenth century, new means of transportation have reduced travel time and increased the pace of economic and cultural globalization. Although major safety improvements have been enacted in recent decades, modern trains, cars, and airplanes are also involved in accidents that kill thousands of people annually. More people travel now than ever before in human history, which helps feed the fear of transportation accidents. These trends have increased pressure on national states to regulate the transportation sector to reduce casualties and to make users of modern transportation feel safer.

Modern auto safety regulation in the United States during the 1960s and 1970s emerged from grassroots mobilization. In his 1965 book *Unsafe at Any Speed*, consumer advocate Ralph Nader condemned the safety record of the auto industry.[22] In this era when courts made producers increasingly responsible for defective products, the push for auto safety gained momentum, and in 1966 Congress passed the Highway Safety Act and the National Traffic and Motor Vehicle Safety Act, the latter of which gave the federal state extensive regulatory power over motor vehicles.[23] Washington could now impose the implementation of safety features like headrests and safety belts in new cars. The 1970s debate over fuel tank fires in Ford Pintos marked a turning point in the development of auto safety in the United States. Though Ford officials knew that the fuel tanks were prone to explode on impact, they finally addressed the problem and withdrew Pintos from the American market only after several years of court challenges and negative media coverage.[24] This case reinforced the need for state regulation in the field of auto safety.

Today the National Highway Traffic Safety Administration (NHTSA), created in 1970, has great regulatory power over the design of motor vehicles. Among other things, the NHTSA requires automakers to meet certain safety performance standards and install particular safety features in all new cars sold in the United States. Other advanced industrial countries have created similar agencies and regulations to protect drivers, passengers, and pedestrians. But as we have seen, these regulations have a cost, generally passed on to consumers.

As the example of auto safety suggests, transportation safety is a concept that refers to a complex set of policies. First, transportation safety oversees product safety, the enforcement of basic safety standards dealing with vehicle construction and maintenance. Second, transportation safety maintains the safety of roads and other infrastructures such as seaports and airports. Third, transportation safety trains and drug-tests professionals who are responsible for passenger safety. Fourth, transportation safety ensures that drivers and passengers respect laws on using safety belts, obeying speed limits, and driving while impaired.[25] Fifth, transportation safety monitors the handling of chemical products and other hazardous materials during travel. And sixth, transportation safety prevents criminal and terrorist acts that endanger the lives of passengers and crewmembers, thus tying transportation safety to issues of public security.[26]

Because these forms of state intervention are so diverse, most advanced industrial societies rely on many separate agencies to assess transportation risks and to enforce national and international rules and regulations. Like environmental regulation, transportation safety is a field in which many actors collaborate on a regular basis; state officials work closely with transportation experts, private businesses, and international organizations such as the International Transportation Safety Organization (ITSA), especially in countries where the state has privatized airports, airlines, train companies, and roadways.[27] Considering the scope of the economic interests at stake, private businesses have a strong incentive to effect state safety policies that may cost them more money or increase public confidence in their sectors of activity.

Especially since September 11, 2001, aviation safety has become a prominent transportation safety issue, both in the United States and abroad.[28] Aviation safety has a unique threat infrastructure because plane crashes are spectacular and tragic, often involving the simultaneous death of many people. As Roger W. Cobb and David M. Primo note, the anxiety generated by plane crashes also stems from the nature of airline transportation:

> Plane crashes capture our attention because they bring to the fore a fact about flying that is often unexpressed: once the cabin door closes, passengers are at the mercy of the crew and the equipment. By nature, humans are loath to relinquish control over their fate, but that is precisely what travelers do each time they fly.[29]

That said, the focus put on this threat by the public, mass media, and state officials may be out of proportion to its actual probability and consequences:

> The chances of dying in a plane accident [are] much less than in any of the following conditions: excessive heat, excessive cold, snakebites, beestings, lightning, suicide, drowning, firearms, or falls. Plane travel, by comparison, is one of the safest public activities.[30]

The events of September 11, 2001, confirmed that public confidence in the airline industry is frail; airline travel in the United States dropped dramatically after the attacks, forcing some airlines into bankruptcy and prompting widespread job losses.[31] The failure to improve the public's perception of aviation safety and security may still cost the industry billions of dollars. In this policy area, as in food safety, state policies to protect citizens against perceived threats are instrumental to the maintenance of powerful economic interests.

Aviation safety is now tied to the "War on Terror," as authorities and airlines attempt to prevent future hijackings. Though hijackings have been a threat since the first modern attempt in 1931, the attacks on

September 11 showed their catastrophic potential, and they are now perceived as national security threats that the state in collaboration with the aviation industry should work to prevent.[32] In response to global terrorism, many countries have strengthened airport and aircraft security through reinforced airport surveillance and extensive passenger and baggage screening.[33] Chapter Six will explore these issues.

Traditional Forms of State Protection Revisited

As new protective measures arise in response to the risks associated with technological change, traditional forms of state protection are still present in the everyday life of citizens in advanced industrial societies.[34] Two of them, policing and social policy, have confronted fresh challenges in recent decades. The traditional law enforcement issue of how to balance security, the protection of individual rights, and the rehabilitation of criminal offenders remains central to policy debates. In the arena of social policy, both the neoliberal creed (see the discussion of neoliberalism in the next section) and recent economic trends have undermined modern welfare states, which have been under attack since the late 1970s. But despite significant neoliberal cutbacks and restructurings, welfare states have survived and in some policy areas even expanded. Policing and social policy remain central aspects of state protection despite the push to increase the reliance on alternative sources of protection, especially market-based sources like private insurance and security services.

Policing

Protecting citizens against theft and violence is perhaps the oldest and the most fundamental responsibility of the modern state. Personal safety and the ownership of property are at the foundation of capitalism and representative democracy, and without basic security and law enforcement, economic and political order would collapse. The political and economic need for physical protection has been a crucial aspect of Western political philosophy since Thomas Hobbes legitimized the state as the unique source of physical protection whose power must remain absolute.[35] Though liberalism has long emphasized the need to limit the power of the state to protect individual rights, public law enforcement is still the foundation of economic, social, and political order in advanced industrial societies.[36]

The debate over sentencing and rehabilitation—i.e., the attempt to reintroduce former inmates to mainstream society—has long divided citizens, experts, and politicians. Countries vary greatly in handling this issue. In Finland, rehabilitation is thought to be the best way to deal with criminals, and state protection against crime does not lead to a high prison population: "Finland's incarceration rate is just 52 per 100,000 people, less than half Canada's rate of 119 per 100,000 people and a tiny fraction of the US rate of 702."[37] The Finnish state employs only 8,500 police officers to protect a population of about 5 million, whereas the New York City Police Department employs more than 39,000 police officers to protect a population of about 8 million.[38]

In contrast with Finland, American belief in rehabilitation has lost much ground since the 1970s. In the United States, longer sentences for drug-related crimes have generated a massive increase in the prison population. The United States has witnessed the emergence of an "incarceration state" in which rehabilitation has taken a backseat, especially when serious crimes like murder, sexual assault, terrorism, and drug dealing are considered. Minority and human rights advocates oppose this harsh model of punishment for its perceived ethnic and racial biases,[39] and the issue of capital punishment fuels these concerns.[40] As of mid-2003, more than 2 million American citizens were in jail; of this number, almost 900,000 were African Americans. The proportion of African Americans in jail is almost four times higher than their share of the American population.[41]

At the same time, the criminal justice system has been relatively lenient in punishing white-collar crime. The phrase "white-collar crime," coined by American sociologist Edwin Sutherland, refers to crimes perpetrated by citizens of a high social status in the context of their professional activities.[42] Although their widespread negative impact on society is undeniable, white-collar fraud and embezzlement do not always result in prison sentences as lengthy as those stemming from drug trafficking, for example. Cases like the recent Enron scandal intensify the debate over the class bias of the criminal justice system.[43]

In North America as in Western Europe, growing fears about crime and terrorism have favored a rapid expansion of the private security industry. Many states contract out security-related tasks, increasing the role of private guards: "The private companies are increasingly doing jobs that once were done by governments, such as operating prisons, enforcing parking regulations, and providing security in courts."[44] In the United States, where no federal laws regulate the private security business,[45] increased reliance on private security guards has raised concern among the media and policymakers. Many believe that Congress should enact national standards to ensure that the more than one million private guards in the United States are properly trained for their tasks; many states do not require background checks or even minimum training hours for private security guards.[46] Increased regulation of the private security industry has also become an issue in Western Europe.[47] Even when the state contracts out services, it must ensure that the public is well-protected.

Urban crime and delinquency are major sources of collective insecurity in many advanced industrial societies. The threat infrastructure of urban delinquency has four major characteristics. First, urban delinquency, which ranges from bullying and disturbing the peace to car theft and gang violence, can become a significant source of collective insecurity in advanced industrial societies because the vast majority of the population lives in urban and suburban areas.[48] Additionally, many citizens living in rural areas commute to urban centers for work. A large portion of the population is thus exposed to urban delinquency.

Second, because the mass media extensively reports violent crimes, people who are never exposed to serious criminal acts may still feel at risk.[49] The spectacular nature of some criminal activities draws media attention and increases the level of collective insecurity. As we discuss further in Chapter Seven, this creates an opportunity for political leaders to exploit the fear of crime in order to promote an agenda of "law and order."

Third, because urban delinquency is associated with social inequality and, in many countries, with ethnic and racial tensions, specific segments of the population are often perceived as potential threats to social order. In France, for example, young members of ethnic minorities living in deprived suburban neighborhoods are the central figures of the ongoing political debate over urban delinquency.[50]

Fourth, delinquency is often perceived as a moral problem, as the behavior of delinquents is frequently seen as both antisocial and immoral. Punishments for delinquency are sometimes severe because perpetrators are seen as deserving retribution.

Policy responses to delinquency vary among jurisdictions. Over the last two decades, "zero tolerance," a policy model often geared towards the fight against urban delinquency, has become increasingly influential in advanced industrial societies. In this model, law enforcement authorities respond to all recognized crimes, even minor crimes like jaywalking and loitering, and the justice system punishes the offenders. The logic of deterrence here is simple: because minor crimes lead to major crimes, authorities prevent minor crimes from occurring in the first place. During the 1990s, the success of New York mayor Rudolph Giuliani in instituting these policies led to their diffusion across the United States.[51] Zero tolerance policies have also been enacted in many American high schools since the Columbine massacre of April 1999.[52] This "tough" approach to crime is explicitly grounded in traditional moral values such as discipline and personal responsibility.

Zero tolerance has been criticized as a repressive model that implicitly targets minorities and the poor while diverting fiscal resources away from social programs. Despite these arguments, the concept of zero tolerance has gained supporters outside the United States over the last decade, especially in the United Kingdom, France, and the Netherlands.[53] Chapter Seven will explore the interesting French case.

Social Policy

Most welfare states expanded greatly in the prosperous postwar era. Current economic and political trends such as neoliberalism, also known as market liberalism, question social policies enacted during and even before that era. The battles between proponents of neoliberalism and those who seek to preserve or even expand the welfare state have led to major changes in the arena of social policy.[54]

Neoliberalism's rise since the late 1970s seems to have undermined the economic and ideological foundations of the welfare state, especially in the Anglo-American world.[55] Associated with the work of economists Milton Friedman and Friedrich Hayek, neoliberalism, based on the idea that markets are more efficient than states at distributing resources and regulating the economy, promotes the application of market solutions to public policy issues.[56] Prior to the large-scale implementation of modern social programs, "old" liberalism opposed statism and socialism in the name of market efficiency, self-reliance, and rugged individualism.[57] Neoliberalism is an attempt to return to this strict individualistic model. Consequently, in recent decades, neoliberalism has found a massive target in the welfare state.[58]

Generally depicting social programs as an economic burden and a source of welfare dependency, the neoliberal creed holds that these programs must be altered, downsized, or privatized in order to reduce taxes and favor economic prosperity. Furthermore, neoliberalism promotes personal responsibility as an alternative, or the solution, to welfare dependency, and expresses skepticism toward most forms of state intervention.[59] Neoliberal economists and politicians support the development of market-based protection, such as private insurance, which could reduce the need for direct state intervention. In the United States, right-wing libertarianism, the radical defense of personal freedom and market economy promoted by think tanks like the CATO Institute, is an uncompromising form of neoliberalism.[60]

The growing influence of neoliberalism since the 1970s has directly con-tributed to the emergence of the "new politics of the welfare state."[61] This politics is characterized by the enactment of fiscal cutbacks and cost-control measures, and by the establishment of workfare programs, which require welfare recipients to work in exchange for cash benefits, and per-sonal savings plans meant to increase individual responsibility.[62]

Despite the domination of neoliberalism and pressures from business interest groups, this "new politics" has not led to the dismantling of mod-ern welfare states.[63] Large social programs create broad constituencies and vested interests that force even the most conservative politicians to avoid open revolutions in social protection. Still, there has been substantial in-stitutional change in some advanced industrial welfare states since the early 1980s.[64] As demonstrated by the 1996 American welfare reform leg-islation, which imposed strict time limits on most recipients, the state can significantly alter the content of social rights and consequently transform the nature of the public "safety net."

Even though neoliberalism has legitimized cutbacks in key social pro-grams and has successfully pushed for some policy privatization, a strong neoliberal convergence between existing national social policy systems has not materialized. Profound cross-national differences remain in terms of expenditure levels and institutional settings.[65] Beyond these variations, contemporary national states still play a crucial role in redistributing in-come and protecting citizens and workers against economic insecurity.

In spite of this, changing risk patterns related to demographic aging and new labor market and family patterns can undermine the efficiency—and even the relevance—of existing forms of social protection. When the state fails to respond to these new trends, such as the growth in precarious em-ployment and single parenthood, existing social programs become increas-ingly irrelevant as they fail to protect large segments of the population.[66] For example, traditional social insurance programs, designed for full-time workers, do not adequately protect the growing army of part-timers. In the United States, Conservative forces dominant in Congress from 1994 to 2006 prevented the enactment of social programs that could have fought grow-ing economic insecurity related to the multiplication of part-time jobs and single-parent families, as well as the stagnation of blue-collar wages.[67]

In some countries, however, the onset of new social risks favors the en-actment of significant measures designed to address emerging socioeco-nomic needs.[68] As such, despite the neoliberal push for spending control, policy expansion of the welfare state remains on the agenda in a number of countries. For example, since the late 1990s, Canada has developed new programs to fight child poverty related to changing family and labor mar-ket structures.[69]

Healthcare reform is a major policy issue in many advanced industrial countries. In the United States, where no universal public health insurance coverage is provided, a debate has raged for decades about possible reforms that could extend such coverage. As of 2005, about 45 million Americans were uninsured,[70] though most of the uninsured have access to some emergency care.

As will be discussed in Chapter Eight, being uninsured remains a major source of economic insecurity in the United States.[71] Moreover, this insecurity affects many insured people who could lose benefits as a consequence of unemployment or the termination of their firm's plan.[72] Those who count on private health insurance also worry about the increase in premium costs. Because many potential voters are concerned with healthcare coverage, it is a recurring issue on the federal policy and electoral agenda.

The threat infrastructure of health insurance policy differs greatly from the other three policy areas discussed here. At the collective level, gaps in healthcare coverage are a slow-moving, structural problem, far less spectacular and concentrated than criminal acts, plane crashes, or even food poisoning epidemics. In healthcare, unlike the three other protection areas, individuals have an intimate and generally accurate perception of the risks of unemployment and being uninsured. As with issues of crime and delinquency, health coverage is directly related to social inequality, which means that politicians can focus on the fate of particular groups at the expense of others. The case of health insecurity has great significance in terms of social inequality and the ways in which the political leaders frame and respond to economic insecurity. This is why Chapter Eight is entirely devoted to this crucial issue.

Despite strong economic, fiscal, and ideological pressures that call for privatization and tight budget controls, citizens' enduring reliance on the state is clear. However, policies supported by proponents of neoliberalism and globalization have had a real impact on state protection. As will be shown in the next chapter, the modern state now faces serious challenges, and policy restructuring remains on the agenda of most advanced industrial societies.

Notes

1. As discussed in Part II, economic and technological forces take on political meaning only when social and political actors construct them as "problems" that the state must address.

2. Ulrich Beck (1992), *Risk Society* (London: Sage Publications), p. 20.
3. See T. Hugh Pennington (2003), *When Food Kills: BSE, E. Coli and Disaster Science* (Oxford: Oxford University Press), and Zhores A. Medvedev (1992), *The Legacy of Chernobyl* (New York: W. W. Norton).
4. Jane Franklin, ed. (1998), *The Politics of Risk Society* (London, Polity Press/IPPR, 1998).
5. Beck, *Risk Society*. The case of nuclear waste supports the above claim about the enduring role of the modern state in the field of environmental protection; see Chuck McCutcheon (2002), *Nuclear Reactions: The Politics of Opening a Radioactive Waste Disposal Site* (Albuquerque: University of New Mexico Press).
6. For example, the Kyoto Protocol on climate change exists only because some national states agreed to comply with it, and the decision of American President George W. Bush not to sign the Protocol strongly reduced the scope of that transnational regulatory model. See Robert S. Devine (2004), *Bush and the Environment* (New York: Random House).
7. Though the House of Representatives finally opposed this measure in November 2005, Republican leadership maintained this unpopular issue on its agenda. See the Associated Press (2005), "Alaska Oil-Drilling Measure May Rise Again," *New York Times*, November 15.
8. Data gathered from the International Atomic Energy Agency (IAEA; available online at www.iaea.org/programmes/a2 [accessed March 2007]).
9. For an overview of the Three Mile Island accident and its consequences, see the United States Nuclear Regulatory Commission Fact Sheet on the Three Mile Island Accident (Washington, DC: Office of Public Affairs; available online at www.nrc.gov/reading-rm/doc-collections/fact-sheets/3mile-isle.html [accessed March 2007]).
10. On Chernobyl, see David R. Marples (1996), "Nuclear Politics in Soviet and Post-Soviet Europe" in John Byrne and Stephen M. Hoffman, eds., *Governing the Atom: The Politics of Risk* (New Brunswick: Transaction Publishers), pp. 247–269, and Medvedev (1992), *The Legacy of Chernobyl*.
11. Madeleine Ferrières (2005), *Sacred Cow, Mad Cow: A History of Food Fear* (New York: Columbia University Press), p. viii. The discussion of this issue draws on Ferrières's book.
12. Ferrières, *Sacred Cow, Mad Cow*.
13. Upton Sinclair (1906, rpt. 1960), *The Jungle* (New York: Signet).
14. On the history of the FDA, see Philip J. Hilts (2005), *Protecting America's Health: The FDA, Business, and One Hundred Years of Regulation* (Chapel Hill: University of North Carolina Press).
15. Grace Skogstad (2003), *Regulating Food Safety Risks in the European Union and North America: Distinctive Regulatory Policy Styles*, paper presented in

November 2003 at the conference "European Food Safety Regulation: The Challenge of Multi-Level Governance" (University of California, Berkeley), p. 2.

16. On the relationship between food supply and globalization, see Peter Atkins and Ian Bowler (2001), *Food in Society: Economy, Culture, Geography* (New York: Oxford University Press).

17. For more discussion on this topic, see Chapter Five.

18. U.S. Department of Agriculture (2001), *Food and Agricultural Policy: Taking Stock for the New Century* (Washington, DC, Government Printing Office; available online at www.usda.gov/news/pubs/farmpolicy01/ fpindex.htm [accessed March 2007]), p. 65.

    Beyond the formal political arena, the scientific field is the site of power struggles between scientists; see Pierre Bourdieu (2004), *Science of Science and Reflexivity* (Chicago: University of Chicago Press).

19. EFSA (2004), "About EFSA" (available online at www.efsa.europa.eu/ en/about_efsa.html [accessed March 2007]).

20. Skogstad, *Regulating Food Safety Risks*.

21. Chapter Five discusses the threat infrastructure of food safety through an analysis of the British debate over BSE.

22. Ralph Nader (1965), *Unsafe at Any Speed: The Designed-In Dangers of the American Automobile* (New York: Grossman).

23. For a brief overview of the history of auto safety in the United States, see Matthew T. Lee (1998), "The Ford Pinto and the Development of Auto Safety Regulations, 1893–1978," *Business and Economic History* 27(2): 390–401.

24. For more on the Pinto case, see Douglas Birsch and John H. Fielder, eds. (1994), *The Ford Pinto Case: A Study in Applied Ethics, Business, and Technology* (Stony Brook: State University of New York Press); Lee Patrick Strobel (1980), *Reckless Homicide? Ford's Pinto Trial* (South Bend, IN: and books); and Francis T. Cullen and Willaim J. Maakestad (1987), *Corporate Crime Under Attack: The Ford Pinto Case and Beyond* (Cincinnati, OH: Anderson).

25. As suggested in Chapter One, citizens may perceive this aspect of transportation safety, the enforcement of these laws, as infringement on personal freedom.

26. For more on issues of security, see Kathleen M. Sweet (2003), *Aviation and Airport Security: Terrorism and Safety Concerns* (New York: Prentice Hall).

27. See Simon Hakim, Paul Seidenstat, and Gary W. Bowman (1996), *Privatizing Transportation Systems* (Westport, CT: Praeger).

28. Aviation safety is discussed in greater detail in Chapter Six.

29. Cobb and Primo (2003), *The Plane Truth: Airline Crashes, the Media, and Transportation Policy* (Washington, DC: Brookings Institutions Press), p. 2.

30. Ibid., p. 155.

31. For more on the impact of the September 11, 2001 attacks on the aviation industry, see Chris Isidore (2006), "Airlines Still in Upheaval, Five Years after 9/11," CNNMoney.com (available online at money. cnn.com/2006/09/08/news/companies/airlines_sept11/?post version=2006090812 [accessed March 2007]); and Mark Tran (2001),"The Airline Industry Slump," *Guardian*, September 20 (available online at www.guardian.co.uk/september11/story/0,11209,601459,00. html [accessed March 2007]).

32. Tran, "The Airline Industry Slump." See also Phillip A. Karber (2002), "Re-constructing Global Aviation in an Era of the Civil Aircraft as a Weapon of Destruction," *Harvard Journal of Law & Public Policy* 25: 781–814; Joseph S. Szyliowicz (2004), "Aviation Security: Promise or Reality?" *Studies in Conflict & Terrorism*, 27(1): 47–63; Joseph S. Szyliowicz (2004), "International Transportation Security," *Review of Policy Research* 21(3):351–368.

33. Sweet, *Aviation and Airport Security*.

34. Technological change affects policing and social policy as well. For example, in the field of policing, the development of security cameras and other surveillance technologies has raised many concerns about privacy. For a general discussion about privacy and surveillance technologies, see David Lyon (2003), *Surveillance after September 11* (Cambridge: Polity), and Mark Monmonier (2002), *Spying with Maps: Surveillance Technologies and the Future of Privacy* (Chicago: University of Chicago Press).

35. Thomas Hobbes (1660, rpt. 1985), *Leviathan* (New York: Penguin). On Hobbes, see M. M. Golschmidt (1966), *Hobbes's Science of Politics* (New York: Columbia University Press), and Corey Robin (2004), *Fear: The History of a Political Idea* (Oxford: Oxford University Press).

36. For a historical perspective on criminal justice and law enforcement, see Lawrence M. Friedman (1994), *Crime and Punishment in American History* (New York: Basic Books).

37. Dan Gardner (2002), "Why Finland Is Soft on Crime," *Ottawa Citizen*, March 18 (available online at www.dangardner.ca/Archmar1802.html [accessed March 2007]).

38. New York City Police Department FAQ page (2004), www.nyc.gov/ html/nypd/html/misc/pdfaq2.html#41 (accessed March 2007).

39. Bruce Western (2006), *Punishment and Inequality in America* (New York: Russell Sage Foundation).

Reluctant to adopt either the Finnish or the American model, countries like Canada have attempted to strike a balance between rehabilitation and retribution; see Dan Gardner (2002), "Why Getting Tough on Crime Failed in the U.S.," *Ottawa Citizen*, May 28.

40. Michael Tonry (1994), *Malign Neglect: Race, Crime, and Punishment in America* (New York: Oxford University Press).

41. Paige M. Harrison and Jennifer C. Karberg (2004), *Prison and Jail Inmates at Midyear 2003* (Washington, DC: Bureau of Justice Statistics Bulletin; available online at www.ojp.usdoj.gov/bjs/abstract/pjim03. htm [accessed March 2007]).

42. Edwin H. Sutherland (1940), "The White-Collar Criminal," *American Sociological Review* 5(1): 1–12.

43. Revealed to the public in late 2001, this scandal involved systematic accounding fraud that untimately led to the bankruptcy of Enron, a Houston-based American energy company.

44. Barry James (2002), "Terrorism Fuels Growth in an Industry Virtually Free of Regulation," *International Herald Tribune*, January 10 (available online at www.iht.com/articles/2002/01/10/guard_ed3_.php [accessed March 2007]).

45. Mimi Hall (2003), "Private Security Guards are Homeland's Weak Link," *USA Today*, January 22 (available online at www.usatoday.com/news/nation/2003-01-22-security-cover_x.htm [accessed March 2007]).

46. Ibid.

47. James, "Terrorism Fuels Growth in an Industry Virtually Free of Regulation."

48. Between 1950 and 2005, for example, the percentage of people living in Canadian and American urban areas increased from 64 to 81 percent; Population Division of the Department of Economic and Social Affairs of the United Nations Secretariat, "World Population Prospects: The 2002 Revision and World Urbanization Prospects: The 2003 Revision, August 23" (esa.un.org/unup [accessed March 2007]).

49. On this issue, see Joel Best (1999), *Random Violence: How We Talk About New Crimes and New Victims* (Berkeley: University of California Press); Barry Glassner (1999), *The Culture of Fear: Why Americans Are Afraid of the Wrong Things* (New York: Basic Books); and Esther Madriz (1997), *Nothing Bad Happens to Good Girls: Fear of Crime in Women's Lives* (Berkeley: University of California Press).

50. For more on this issue, see Chapter Seven.

51. In New York, the implementation of strict zero tolerance policies has raised concerns about police brutality and the excessive use of force in law enforcement; see Andrea McArdle and Tanya Erzen, eds. (2001), *Zero Tolerance: Quality of Life and the New Police Brutality in New York City* (New York: New York University Press).

52. Ronnie Casella (2001), *At Zero Tolerance: Punishment, Prevention, and School Violence* (New York: Peter Lang Publishing).
53. Loïc Wacquant (1999), *Les Prisons de la misère* (Paris: Raisons d'agir).
54. Paul Pierson (1994), *Dismantling the Welfare State? Reagan, Thatcher, and the Politics of Retrenchment* (Cambridge: Cambridge University Press). See also Gøsta Esping-Andersen (1996), *Welfare States in Transition: National Adaptation in Global Economies* (London: Sage).

    An increasing number of scholars reject the idea of a "frozen" welfare state; see Wolfgan Streeck and Kathleen Thelen, eds. (2005), *Beyond Continuity: Institutional Change in Advanced Political Economies* (Oxford: Oxford University Press).
55. This discussion of neoliberalism draws on Daniel Béland, "Insecurity, Citizenship, and Globalization: The Multiple Faces of State Protection," *Sociological Theory* 23(1) 2005: 25–41.
56. See John Campbell and Ove Kaj Pedersen, eds., (2001), *The Rise of Neoliberalism and Institutional Analysis* (Princeton: Princeton University Press), and David Harvey (2005), *A Brief History of Neoliberalism* (Oxford: Oxford University Press).
57. C. B. MacPherson (1962), *The Political Theory of Possessive Individualism* (Oxford: Clarendon Press).
58. This conflict is already apparent in Friedrich von Hayek's revolutionary 1944 book *The Road to Serfdom* (London: Routledge & Kegan Paul).
59. Margaret Somers and Fred Block (2005), "From Poverty to Perversity: Ideational Embeddedness and the Rise and Reprise of Market Liberalism," *American Sociological Review* 70(2): 260–287.
60. On libertarianism, see George H. Nash (1976, rpt. 1996), *The Conservative Intellectual Movement in America since 1945* (Wilmington, DE: Intercollegiate Studies Institute).
61. Pierson, *Dismantling the Welfare State?*
62. On workfare, see Robert H. Cox (1998), "The Consequences of Welfare Reform: How Conceptions of Social Rights are Changing," *Journal of Social Policy* 27(1): 1–16.

    On personal savings, see Daniel Béland (2007), *History and Politics from the New Deal to the Privatization Debate*, Paperback Edition with New Afterword (Lawrence: University Press of Kansas), and Jill Quadagno (1999), "Creating a Capital Investment Welfare State," *American Sociological Review* 64(1): 1–10.
63. Paul Pierson, ed. (2001), *The New Politics of the Welfare State* (Oxford: Oxford University Press).

    Economic insecurity is still a central preoccupation in contemporary societies; see John Vail, Michael J. Hill, and Jane Wheelock (1999), *Insecure Times: Living with Insecurity in Contemporary Society* (London: Routledge).

64. See, for example, John Myles and Paul Pierson (1997), "Friedman's Revenge: The Reform of 'Liberal' Welfare States in Canada and the United States," *Politics and Society* 25(4): 443–472.

65. Duane Swank (2002), *Global Capital, Political Institutions, and Policy Change in Developed Welfare States* (Cambridge: Cambridge University Press).

    For an alternative view on convergence, see Neil Gilbert (2002), *Transformation of the Welfare State: The Silent Surrender of Public Responsibility* (Oxford: Oxford University Press).

66. This is what Jacob Hacker calls "policy drift." See Hacker (2004), "Privatizing Risk without Privatizing the Welfare State: The Hidden Politics of Social Policy Retrenchment in the United States," *American Political Science Review* 98(2): 243–260.

67. For a discussion on the negative effects of this situation see Jacob S. Hacker (2006), *The Great Risk Shift* (New York: Oxford University Press).

68. Peter Taylor-Gooby, ed. (2004), *New Risks, New Welfare: The Transformation of the European Welfare State* (Oxford: Oxford University Press).

69. See Jane Jenson (2004), "Changing the Paradigm: Family Responsibility or Investing in Children," *Canadian Journal of Sociology* 29(2): 169–192, and James J. Rice and Michael J. Prince (2000), *Changing Politics of Canadian Social Policy* (Toronto: University of Toronto Press).

70. See Chapter Eight for more on this topic.

71. Hacker, *The Great Risk Shift*.

72. On this issue see Jill Quadagno (2005), *One Nation, Uninsured* (New York: Oxford University Press).

3

Does Globalization Matter?

Globalization is a trend that affects our daily lives, yet there is no consensus on what effects it has on state protection. Recent commentary and scholarship argue that economic and social transformations related to globalization favor a strong decline of state power and the emergence of a new global political order.[1] As argued in this chapter, this view is misleading: the rise of globalization does not necessarily indicate a decline in the power of the state. However, the challenges of globalization may make citizens feel insecure and complicate state protection. Globalization thus has serious consequences, as factors related to it, such as global terrorism and environmental challenges, generate new fears and protection demands.

Some current literature on globalization, such as the works of Manuel Castells, argues that this trend has a negative impact on the national state. As we will see, national fiscal choices, more than constraints associated with global capitalism, may affect state protection. The bold income tax cuts enacted during George W. Bush's first term support this claim: as they helped build large federal deficits in a time of increased defense spending, these cuts depleted the fiscal resources available to create new social or environmental programs. Because of the relationship between state protection and fiscal extraction, major tax cuts and the budget deficits they can create are perhaps the most direct threat to state protection in advanced industrial societies. Without adequate fiscal resources, the state cannot meet its complex protection tasks. This reality points to the autonomy of political leaders like President George W. Bush who promote the neoliberal project and who choose to reduce income taxes for political and ideological reasons.

As for globalization, this chapter suggests that global trends increase perceived protection needs and, in some cases, reliance on the national state. In addition to global terrorism, issues of economic globalization and immigration illustrate that global forces and the discourse on globalization may help generate collective insecurity.[2] Thorough analysis of these issues points to the enduring role of political leaders in the construction of collective insecurity and the making—and unmaking—of state protection.

Defining Globalization

Although the modern concept of globalization is relatively recent,[3] globalization itself is not a new phenomenon. From the conquest of the New World during the Renaissance to the first campaign for free trade in the nineteenth century, globalization is sometimes viewed as a consequence of technological change and modern capitalism.[4] Globalization is a crucial part of modernity, and over the last few decades its long-term economic and social processes have intensified.[5]

Like many popular concepts, globalization takes on different meanings in social science literature. Since the 1980s, social scientists have debated the impact of globalization on the modern state and the contemporary world. Much of this literature focuses on globalization's negative impact; from this perspective, global trade and finance, as well as international organizations propagating the neoliberal creed, work together to weaken the power of the modern state:

> [T]ransnational corporations (TNCs) seem ever more able to evade the reach of state regulation. The policies and activities of the World Trade Organization (WTO) and the International Monetary Fund (IMF) are frequently seen as interfering with the sovereignty and autonomy of states and promoting a global corporate agenda.[6]

This pessimistic vision of economic globalization, shared by many left-wing academics, advocates, and public intellectuals, is based on the assumption that global capitalism increases economic inequality and social insecurity around the world. Those who hold this view

> regard globalization as the tool multinational corporations are using to rob the world's poor by exploiting their labour, resources, and environments, destroying their cultures, and commanding their vassal governments to implement whatever laws and trade agreements would make these transfers easier to achieve.[7]

In contrast to this sharp critique of neoliberal globalization, many economists and chambers of commerce, as well as right-wing journalists and politicians, disseminate a more optimistic discourse on the "global economy." This discourse stresses the rewards of transnational markets and investments: "globaphiles are convinced that universal market openness is the single most vital key to higher living standards."[8]

Beyond these competing visions of economic globalization, some authors emphasize the technological and ideological forces related to globalization. For example, these forces compress time and space, thus increasing the scope of transnational exchanges. From this perspective, a growing world economy is only one aspect of globalization: "globalization is a process fueled by, and resulting in, increasing cross-border flows of goods, services, money, people, information, and culture."[9] Such cross-border flows create a "shrinking of the world."[10]

Before exploring these issues, we should define globalization. As our discussion shows, it can be understood in many ways, but its vagueness should not lead us to reject the concept altogether or to believe that formulating a coherent definition for it is impossible.[11] Most definitions of globalization are not insightful because they reduce globalization to well-known processes like internationalization and Westernization. A good definition of globalization should instead generate new insights about the world in which we live.

International relations scholar Jan Aart Scholte defines globalization as "the spread of transplanetary . . . connections between people. From this perspective, globalization involves reductions in barriers to transworld contacts."[12] These contacts include global migrations, financial flows, civil society organizations, and communication networks like the Internet, all of which help to create "one world."[13] Data about foreign direct investment (FDI), investment made by a foreign firm or individual in another country's economy, illustrate the acceleration of this process: between 1990 and 2001, such investment increased from $1.7 to $6.6 trillion, and since the 1960s, the number of transnational firms has increased from 7,000 to more than 65,000.[14] But though these data suggest that economic globalization is a powerful and influential process, we should recognize that "territorial geography continues to have importance alongside the new supranationality . . . globalization is not intrinsically a culturally homogenizing process . . . global relations have spread unevenly across regions and social sectors . . . [and] globalization is a thoroughly political question. . . ."[15]

Globalization is a political issue with uneven effects and consequences. The following section will support the claim that globalization has not favored a major decline of state power in advanced industrial societies.

Globalization and the Resilience of State Power

Despite growing evidence that contradicts their claims, several prominent contemporary thinkers argue that globalization favors a decline of the national state.[16] According to Michael Hardt and Antonio Negri, for example, the world is witnessing the emergence of a global capitalist "Empire"

in which national states have a far less central position than before.[17] Discourse on the decline of the national state, though shared across ideological lines, is especially popular on the far left, where Marxists and former Marxists have long promoted internationalism and the revolt of the "multitude" (i.e., ordinary people) against global capitalism.[18]

For sociologist Manuel Castells, the planetary expansion of information networks like the Internet goes against national institutions and hierarchies:

> Networks dissolve centres, they disorganize hierarchy. . . . Thus, contemporary information networks of capital, production, trade, science, communication, human rights, and crime, bypass the national state, which, by and large, has stopped being a sovereign entity.[19]

From this perspective, the development of global capitalism and new communication technologies makes national states increasingly irrelevant: in a world of global communication, national boundaries lose their meaning.

However, these views oversimplify globalization's impact on the national state. Far from being passive in the process of globalization, policymakers in advanced industrial countries often promote free trade, economic integration, and foreign investment in order to gain electoral power and to push their own political agendas at home. These actors stress the domestic prosperity that can result from global exchange: economic openness may benefit countries and may even stimulate welfare state development and coordination. In Canada, for example, the Liberal Party in power between 1993 and 2006 promoted economic integration through the North American Free Trade Agreement (NAFTA) while stressing the need to preserve and even improve the country's welfare state. This welfare state was reframed as a competitive tool oriented toward the reproduction of a well-educated and competitive workforce.[20]

The enactment of NAFTA and, more significant, the creation of the European Union (EU), are the most spectacular outcomes of the integration strategy many political leaders have initiated. Yet institutional and political integration remains limited even within the EU; for example, national states remain in charge of the large social insurance systems that protect workers and citizens against economic insecurity. As such, national states remain the primary source of economic, environmental, social, and military protection in advanced industrial societies.

Consequently, the role of the state is enduring—and even increasing—in advanced industrial societies, despite international variations in taxes and public spending levels.[21] Since 2001, increased public awareness of terrorism in these societies has reinforced the state's legitimacy as the main source of security; when facing the threat of global terrorism, citizens and private businesses like the aviation industry turn to the state for

Table 3.1

**State Real Expenditure, 1937–1995
(as a percentage of GDP)**

	1937	1960	1980	1990	1995
Canada	10.1	13.4	19.2	19.8	19.6
France	15.0	14.2	18.1	18.0	19.3
Italy	. . .	12.0	14.7	17.4	16.3
Germany	21.0	13.4	20.2	18.4	19.5
Spain	10.7	8.3	12.5	15.5	16.6
Sweden	10.4	16.0	29.3	27.4	25.8
United Kingdom	11.7	16.4	21.6	20.6	21.4
United States	12.9	19.4	18.7	18.9	16.2

Source: Tanzi and Schuknecht, *Public Spending in the 20th Century*, p. 25.

protection.[22] Considering this, as well as the long-term trends of public spending (see Table 3.1), economic globalization has not caused a massive decline of state power. These trends in public spending suggest that, in the advanced industrial world, national states remain massive actors involved in a number of complex and expensive tasks. Recent scholarship on the national state strengthens the claim that it can still implement policies that strongly affect the life of its citizens.[23]

We should keep in mind three precautionary remarks about globalization and the resilience of state power. First, what is true of advanced industrial societies does not necessarily apply to other parts of the world. In many former socialist countries, for example, the departure from economic planning, widespread neoliberal reforms, and the expansion of organized crime and the informal economic sector (i.e., activities that are neither taxed nor regulated by the legal system) have temporarily reduced the state's capacity to extract fiscal resources and protect citizens. Declining or insufficient state protection and growing collective insecurity stimulate the development of alternative providers of protection like militias and criminal organizations. This happened in Russia before and immediately after the collapse of the Soviet Union in 1991,[24] suggesting that a strong decline in state power is possible, and that globalization is not necessarily the main factor behind it.

Second, state protection is not an institutional "status quo." Even in advanced industrial countries, state protection may not expand, or even maintain itself, indefinitely. Across countries and policy areas, neoliberal cutbacks and restructuring have reduced the concrete level of state protection offered without any influence from the global economy. The drastic 1996 American welfare reform (discussed in Chapter Two) is an example of the decline of state protection in a specific policy area. Furthermore, in analyzing changes in the level of state protection, we must distinguish between political rhetoric about protection and the concrete reforms that have been enacted. For example, "social democratic" rhetoric may have hidden the true scope of cutbacks and restructuring that have significantly altered—and even reduced the level of—state protection in countries like Denmark and Sweden.[25]

Third, domestic policy decisions may shrink a state's fiscal resources through the enactment of widespread income tax breaks, which in the long run may seriously reduce the state's capacity to protect citizens effectively. Because protection capacity is tied to fiscal revenues, and because income tax cuts are politically difficult to overturn, fiscal crises triggered by deep income tax breaks represent a potential menace to state protection. The deficits incurred by these tax breaks may legitimize budget cuts in social and environmental programs, and may lead to the multiplication of alternative, market-based providers of protection. This situation may then lead to increased social inequality, as market-based protection tends to cover more affluent citizens.[26]

The United States is probably the main advanced industrial country where a large-scale fiscal crisis is most likely to have a negative impact on state protection. The massive federal income tax cuts enacted in 2001 and 2003 have already led to the return of mammoth federal deficits.[27] Though these tax cuts were ostensibly enacted as temporary measures, political pressure to make them permanent is strong,[28] even in light of the new protection demands created by the 2005 Katrina catastrophe in New Orleans.[29] In the future, fiscal crises related to these tax cuts could justify bolder budget cuts and reduce the federal state's capacity to effectively fight threats from economic insecurity and environmental hazards to international terrorism.

The United States faces a deepening contradiction between limited tax revenues and rising protection needs;[30] elected officials who promote the economic interests of specific, frequently narrow, constituencies[31] have significantly reduced the capacity of the state to raise revenues, while greatly increasing military spending and breeding fears concerning global terrorism.[32] Fighting terrorism, environmental threats, and economic insecurity is increasingly expensive, and a growing number of citizens may soon discover that cutting income taxes—especially those of the wealthy—diminishes the state's capacity to protect society against the threats that concern them.

As we have discussed, state protection involves major tradeoffs and necessitates setting fiscal and policy priorities. Income tax cuts and budget deficits are thus a major aspect of the debate over the future of state protection, in the United States and abroad. The state must raise enough taxes to finance appropriate policy responses to growing protection demands. But who should pay for such expanding protection? This is a difficult *political* question, as setting fiscal priorities and tax levels is largely about power relations.

New Protection Needs

Globalization itself has not greatly reduced the capacity of the modern state to protect its citizens. However, globalization has definitely affected state protection and the politics of insecurity in two main ways.

Complicating the Actions of the State

First, global trends may complicate or undermine the actions of the state regarding economic, social, or environmental insecurity. For example, pressures from global trade, capital markets, and production create fiscal constraints for policymakers who seek to attract foreign investment and to prevent companies from relocating to other countries. European monetary integration, an example of economic globalization, has forced EU member states to adopt strict budget policies that have reduced their capacity to enact new protection programs, or even to finance existing ones.[33] Financial globalization and competition for foreign investment have also increased the political leverage of business interests, which tend to oppose constraining labor regulations and high corporate and payroll taxes.[34] With the internationalization of protection, the increasingly common idea that firms could relocate to another country "gives more leverage to capital and thus puts downward pressures on employer contributions to welfare state programs and on corporate taxation."[35] This increase in business power may also give more momentum to neoliberal campaigns aimed at privatizing—or downsizing—significant components of state protection. Where the welfare state is concerned, however, evidence shows that national actors and institutions still matter a great deal and that economic globalization has not favored strong institutional convergence.[36]

Regarding the environment, the effects of air and water pollution are increasingly global in nature, and it is difficult for national states to act alone to fight these global environmental threats. Cooperation between states thus becomes necessary.[37] As suggested in Chapter Two, environmental and economic globalization can reinforce each other, as in the field of food safety. In that policy area, global trade can facilitate the propagation of food hazards like BSE while creating new trade conflicts.[38]

Growing Protection Demands

Second, globalization and the social, economic, and environmental fears it triggers can lead to new protection demands in society,[39] as is clearly the case with global terrorism. In the past, local and regional terrorist networks challenged the authority of the national state in countries, as in Spain (Basque Country) and the United Kingdom (Northern Ireland).[40] In recent decades, new communication technologies and increased transnational mobility have accelerated the development of global terrorist networks, making them difficult to detect and dismantle;[41] to do so, national states rely on intelligence and international cooperation. The global nature of contemporary terrorist networks has complicated the role of the state, but has simultaneously reinforced its legitimacy as the main provider of protection. The strong reliance of the United States on the FBI, the CIA, and the recently created Department of Homeland Security to fight terrorist threats provides ground to this claim. Still, collaboration between these federal agencies and foreign state agencies like Britain's Secret Intelligence Service (SIS) is increasingly common.

Economic globalization can complicate or undermine the actions of the state, but it can also justify more comprehensive state protection. As workers from advanced industrial countries fear downsizing and international production relocation stemming from globalization, they depend more on the national state for economic security; paradoxically, global trade and finance aggravate economic insecurity, which in turn make the national state the only stable source of protection against global insecurity.

In advanced industrial societies, political leaders can use the insecurity associated with economic globalization to appeal to voters and to justify the policy alternatives they champion. During the 2004 American presidential campaign, for example, Democratic candidate John Kerry referred often to economic globalization as a source of collective insecurity that the federal state should fight.[42] For Kerry, this insecurity was a challenge that the state can confront, not an irremediable source of state decline. Despite the emergence of global social movements that challenge neoliberal globalization and promote alternative, transnational forms of governance and solidarity,[43] many national political leaders still depict themselves as genuine defenders of ordinary citizens against the (perceived) negative effects of economic globalization.

Immigration, a symbol of globalization also remains an enduring source of concern and protection demands. In many advanced industrial countries, national identity is deeply rooted in common languages and culture.[44] In these countries, immigrants may become scapegoats for the social and economic problems that citizens link to globalization. During the last two decades, far-right parties have exploited economic insecurity and urban delinquency to gain support from insecure voters who believe that immigrants are the source of these problems. In countries as varied as Austria, Belgium, Denmark, France, the Netherlands, and Switzerland, populist, far-right parties have depicted immigrants and their children as threatening national values and institutions; for these xenophobic parties, the state must protect national societies from "excessive levels" of immigration and globalization.[45] When depicted as a threat to national identity, globalization can thus strengthen the protective mission of the state, but in this context protection applies only to native-born citizens, not to immigrants and their children. Although xenophobia is not a new phenomenon, politically manipulated fears associated with globalization and transnational migrations can legitimize a potentially repressive form of state protection.

The global spread of diseases such as BSE, SARS, and "bird flu" is another growing source of collective insecurity in advanced industrial countries. Because of their potential to sicken millions of citizens, these diseases receive much media attention, and as a result, global disease has become a key political issue.

Bird flu (avian influenza) presents a striking example of the relationship between global disease and collective insecurity. Especially since 2003, the public has been acutely aware of this potential pandemic threat. At the pinnacle of media buzz on this issue in late 2005, birds became the symbol of a health threat that propagates beyond national borders. As with BSE, bird flu has also presented political leaders with opportunities to depict themselves as competent risk fighters devoted to public safety and security. For example, in November 2005 President Bush used this issue to portray himself as a responsive politician able to cope with potential national and global emergencies.[46] This helped the president to divert attention from the Hurricane Katrina catastrophe, during which many journalists and politicians accused his administration of responding slowly to emergencies.[47]

Global issues like those discussed above create new anxieties and, for that reason, feed national debates about state protection and collective insecurity. Although globalization is clearly an important trend, variations between countries remain strong and the national states remain the enduring focal point of the politics of insecurity. Interestingly, however, global trends and the discourse about them are playing a growing political role within many of these national states. Part II of this book will provide more ground to this claim.

Conclusion to Part I

From a global and historical perspective, we can grasp the increasing complexity and the enduring character of state protection in advanced industrial societies. As discussed in Chapter One, our understanding of state protection must consider the relationship between the state and alternative providers of protection, as well as potential tradeoffs between personal freedom and collective security. Furthermore, while economic and technological forces are instrumental in the development of state protection, only when these forces take on a political meaning do social and political actors present them as collective problems that the state must address in order to reduce insecurity. As suggested in Chapter Two, and as we will see in the four case studies presented in Part II, the construction of collective insecurity is grounded in a threat infrastructure that varies, sometimes considerably, from one policy area to another.

A growing number of social scientists agree that globalization has not strongly undermined the capacity of the state to protect citizens against an increasing amount of national and global threats. That said, globalization can significantly affect state protection, as it aggravates collective insecurity and complicates the state's protective missions. Beyond globalization itself, the political discourse about perceived global threats can exacerbate collective insecurity and create new protection demands. Still, despite the emergence of transnational forms of governance in policy areas like aviation safety, food safety, and pollution control, the national state remains the most crucial provider of collective protection in advanced industrial societies.

Regardless of the safeguards that have emerged as part of modern, liberal citizenship, state power can still become an oppressive force in contemporary societies. Particularly when addressing issues like crime and national security, state protection remains the ambiguous and potentially repressive political construction that Charles Tilly described. State protection, therefore, cannot be idealized, and the actions of the state are not always positive.

State protection is an ambiguous and potentially repressive political construction. Following Tilly, one can argue that this is true in part because political actors participate actively in the construction of collective threats. Part II will venture further inside the politics of insecurity to analyze how these actors are directly involved in the construction of collective insecurity surrounding state protection.

Notes

1. Oddly, the argument that globalization is a major challenge to state power is more prevalent in sociology and social theory literature than in political science.
2. On the idea that globalization is also a discourse, see Colin Hay and Ben Rosamond (2002), "Globalization, European Integration and the Discursive Construction of Economic Imperatives," *Journal of European Public Policy* 9(2): 147–67.
3. American economist Theodore Levitt coined the term in his 1983 article "The Globalization of Markets," *Harvard Business Review,* May–June.
4. See, for example, Immanuel Wallerstein (1974), *The Modern World-System* (New York: Academic Press).
5. Anthony Giddens (1990), *The Consequences of Modernity* (Stanford: Stanford University Press).

   For other long-term historical perspectives on globalization, see Jürgen Osterhammel and Niels Petersson, *Globalization: A Short History* (Princeton: Princeton University Press); Anthony G. Hopkins, ed. (2002), *Globalization in World History* (New York: Random House); Robbie Robertson (2003), *The Three Waves of Globalization: A History of a Developing Global Consciousness* (London, Zed Books); and William I. Robinson, *A Theory of Global Capitalism: Production, Class, and State in a Transnational World* (Baltimore: Johns Hopkins University Press, 2004).

6. Michael Goodhart (2001), "Democracy, Globalization, and the Problem of the State," *Polity* 33(4): 527–46.

   For a strong critique of the IMF, see Joseph E. Stiglitz (2002), *Globalization and Its Discontents* (New York, W. W. Norton).
7. John F. Helliwell (2002), *Globalization and Well-Being* (Vancouver: University of British Columbia Press), p. 78.

   For examples of anti-globalization discourse, see Alex Callinicos (2001), *Against the Third Way: An Anti-Capitalist Critique* (Cambridge: Polity); Noreena Hertz (2002), *The Silent Takeover: Global Capitalism and the Death of Democracy* (New York: Free Press).
8. Helliwell, *Globalization and Well-Being*, p. 78.
9. Mauro F. Guillén (2001), "Is Globalization Civilizing, Destructive or Feeble? A Critique of Six Key Debates in the Social Science Literature," *Annual Review of Sociology* 27: 235–260.
10. James H. Mittelman (1996), "The Dynamics of Globalization" in James H. Mittelman, ed., *Globalization: Critical Reflections* (Boulder: Lynne Rienner), pp. 1–20.
11. Jan Aart Scholte (2002), *What Is Globalization? The Definitional Issue—Again*, Center for the Study of Globalization and Regionalization, GSGR Working Paper No. 109/02 (Coventry: University of Warwick). See also Scholte (2005), *Globalization: A Critical Introduction*, Second Edition (New York: Routledge).
12. Scholte, *What Is Globalization?* pp. 14–15.

   For an alternative definition of globalization centered on the idea of denationalization, see Saskia Sassen (2006), *Territory, Authority, Rights: From Medieval to Global Assemblages* (Princeton: Princeton University Press).
13. On global financial flows, see Robert Gilpin (2000) *The Challenge of Global Capitalism* (Princeton: Princeton University Press); Herman M. Schwartz (2000), *States Versus Markets: The Emergence of a Global Economy*, Second Edition (Houndmills: Palgrave, Macmillan).
14. United Nations Conference on Trade and Development (2002), World Investment Report Overview (New York: United Nations), p. 1.
15. Scholte, *What Is Globalization?* p. 4.
16. This section draws on Daniel Béland, "Insecurity, Citizenship, and Globalization: The Multiple Faces of State Protection," *Sociological Theory* 23(1) 2005: 25–41.
17. Hardt and Negri (2000), *Empire* (Cambridge, MA: Harvard University Press); see also Michael Hardt and Antonio Negri (2004), *Multitude: War and Democracy in the Age of Empire* (New York: Penguin).

   For a review of the growing literature on globalization and the state, see Suzanne Berger (2000), "Globalization and Politics," *Annual Review of Political Science* 3: 43–62; Colin Hay and David Marsh (2000), *Demystifying Globalization* (Houndmills: Palgrave); Scholte, *Globalization*; and Hendrik Spruyt (2002), "The Origins, Development, and Possible Decline of the Modern State," *Annual Review of Political Science* 5: 127–49.

18. For a historical perspective on Marxist internationalism, see R. Craig Nation (1989), *War on War: Lenin, the Zimmerwald Left, and the Origins of Communist Internationalism* (Durham, NC: Duke University Press).

    For other ideologies that agree that the state is gradually weakening because of globalization, see Anthony Giddens (2000), *Runaway World: How Globalization Is Reshaping Our Lives* (New York: Routledge); William Greider (1997), *One World Ready or Not: The Manic Logic of Global Capitalism* (New York: Simon and Schuster); Jean-Marie Guéhenno (1995), *The End of the Nation-State* (Minneapolis: University of Minnesota Press); and Susan Strange (1996), *The Retreat of the State: The Diffusion of Power in the World Economy* (Cambridge: Cambridge University Press).

19. Manuel Castells (2000), "Materials for an Exploratory Theory of the Network Society," *British Journal of Sociology* 51(1): 5–24. For a complete presentation of Castells's ambitious theory, see Castells (1996–1998), *The Information Age: Economy, Society, and Culture*, Three Vols. (Oxford: Blackwell).

20. It is still too soon to tell whether this plan has been successful.

    See James J. Rice and Michael J. Prince (2000), *Changing Politics of Canadian Social Policy* (Toronto: University of Toronto Press); Bruno Théret (2001), "La solidarité sociale dans le pacte fédéral canadien. Histoire d'une crise et de son dénouement," *Critique Internationale*, April: 145–60.

21. On varying tax policies, see OECD (2001), "Challenges for Tax Policy in OECD Countries," *OECD Economic Outlook* 69, June.

    On public spending levels, see Vito Tanzi and Ludger Schuknecht (2000), *Public Spending in the 20th Century: A Global Perspective* (Cambridge: Cambridge University Press).

22. The state must now fight elusive terrorist groups that require the development of reinforced, global intelligence networks. On this issue, see Ulrich Beck (2002), "The Terrorist Threat: World Risk Society Revisited," *Theory, Culture & Society* 19(4): 39–55.

    For more on the aviation industry, see Chapter Six.

23. See, for example, John Campbell (2004), *Globalization and Institutional Change* (Princeton: Princeton University Press); Helliwell, *Globalization and Well-Being*; T. V. Paul, G. John Ikenberry and John Hall, eds. (2003), *The Nation-State in Question* (Princeton: Princeton University Press); and Peter Urmetzer (2005), *Globalization Unplugged: Sovereignty and the*

Canadian State in the 20th Century (Toronto: University of Toronto Press).

The national state remains a crucial aspect of the contemporary world order that exists alongside—and interacts with—global capitalism: see David Harvey (2003), *The New Imperialism* (New York: Oxford University Press).

24. See Diego Gambetta (1993), *The Sicilian Mafia: The Business of Private Protection* (Cambridge: Harvard University Press); William Stanley (1996), *The Protection Racket State: Elite Politics, Military Extortion, and Civil War in El Salvador* (Philadelphia: Temple University Press); and Federico Varese (2001), *The Russian Mafia: Private Protection in a New Market Economy* (Oxford: Oxford University Press); Vadim Volkov (2000), "The Political Economy of Protection Rackets in the Past and the Present," *Social Research* 67(3): 709–744.

    Market providers of protection have also grown in recent years, even in countries like the United States, and these countries have not witnessed a strong decline in state capacity: Bruce L. Benson (1997), "Crime Control Through Private Enterprise," *The Independent Review*, 2(3): 341–371.

25. Robert H. Cox (2004) "The Path Dependence of an Idea: Why Scandinavian Welfare States Remain Distinct," *Social Policy and Administration* 38(2): 204–19.

26. Jacob S. Hacker (2002), *The Divided Welfare State: The Battle over Public and Private Social Benefits in the United States* (Cambridge: Cambridge University Press).

27. James K. Galbraith (2003), "Bush Tax Cuts Will Do a Number on Us," *Newsday*, May 24 (available online at www.commondreams.org/views03/0524-01.htm [accessed March 2007]).

28. William W. Beach (2004), *Make the Temporary Tax Cuts Permanent Tax Reductions*, Heritage Foundation WebMemo #403, January 22 (www.heritage.org/Research/Taxes/wm403.cfm [accessed March 2007]).

29. Jill Lawrence (2005), "Governors Handle Crisis in Own Ways," *USA Today*, September 12 (available online at www.usatoday.com/news/nation/2005-09-12-two-governors_x.htm [accessed March 2007]).

30. This situation is reminiscent of the one prevailing during President Reagan's first term; see Thomas Edsall (1984), *The New Politics of Inequality* (New York: W. W. Norton).

31. The size, structure, and redistribution of the 2001 federal tax cut were at odds with median-voter preferences; this legislation mainly served the interests of the wealthy. See Jacob S. Hacker and Paul Pierson (2005), *Off Center: The Republican Revolution and the Erosion of American Democracy* (New Haven, CT: Yale University Press).

32. On the increase of military spending in the United States, see Dana Milbank and Mike Allen (2003), "Bush to Double Iraq Spending; President Seeks $87 Billion More For Postwar Effort," *Washington Post*, September 8.

33. James I. Walsh (1999), *European Monetary Integration and Domestic Politics in Britain, France, and Italy* (Boulder: Lynne Rienner).

34. Corporate and payroll taxes have a far more direct impact on large businesses than income taxes.

35. Evelyne Huber and John D. Stephens (2001), *Development and Crisis of the Welfare State: Parties and Policies in Global Markets* (Chicago: University of Chicago Press), p. 337.

36. For a critical discussion of this issue, see Campbell, *Institutional Change and Globalization*, and Duane Swank (2002), *Global Capital, Political Institutions, and Policy Change in Developed Welfare States* (Cambridge: Cambridge University Press).

37. Ken Conca and Geoffrey D. Dabelko (1998), *Green Planet Blues: Environmental Politics from Stockholm to Kyoto* (Boulder: Westview Press).

   For an update concerning international agreements in the field of environmental regulation, see Fridtjof Nansens Institutt (2001–2004), *Yearbook of International Co-operation on Environment and Development* (London: Earthscan; see www.fni.no/projects/ybiced.html [accessed March 2007] for a full list of publications under this series title).

38. For more on this issue, see Chapter Five.

39. For a discussion on the relationship between globalization and forms of collective insecurity in developing and advanced industrial countries, see Jose V. Ciprut, ed., (2000) *Of Fears and Foes: Security and Insecurity in an Evolving Global Political Economy* (Westport, CT: Praeger), and Barbara Harris-White, ed. (2002), *Globalization and Insecurity: Political, Economic, and Physical Challenges* (Houndmills: Palgrave).

40. Michael von Tangen Page (1998), *Prisons, Peace and Terrorism: Penal Policy in the Reduction of Political Violence in Northern Ireland, Italy and the Spanish Basque Country, 1968–97* (Houndmills: Palgrave).

41. On the relationship between globalization and terrorism see Beck, "The Terrorist Threat," and Jamal R. Nassar (2004), *Globalization and Terrorism: The Migration of Dreams and Nightmares* (Lanham, MD: Rowman & Littlefield).

42. John Kerry (2004), "A Jobs First Economic Plan," March 26 (www.cfr.org/publication.html?id=6896&issue=18 [accessed March 2007]).

43. Jackie Smith (2004), *Democratizing Globalization? Impacts and Limitations of Transnational Social Movements* (Hamilton: McMaster University Working Paper Series [GHC 04/7]]), December.

44. Globalization has not strongly undermined state and sub-state national identities, which remain strong even within the European Union. On this issue, see Michael Keating and John Mcarry, eds. (2002), *Minority Nationalism and the Changing International Order* (Oxford: Oxford University Press).

45. Hans-Georg Betz (2002), "Against Globalization: Xenophobia, Identity Politics and Exclusionary Populism in Western Europe" in Leo Panitch and Colin Leys, eds., *Fighting Identities: Race, Religion and Ethno-Nationalism* (London: Merlin), pp. 193–210.

    In the United States, the party system seldom allows third parties to develop. This does not mean, however, that anti-immigration sentiments are absent from that country's political debates; see Daniel J. Tichenor (2002), *Dividing Lines: The Politics of Immigration Control in America* (Princeton: Princeton University Press).

46. Gardiner Harris (2005), "Bush Announces Plan to Prepare for Flu Epidemic," *New York Times*, November 2.

47. Richard W. Stevenson and Carl Hulse (2005), "Bush Aide Will Lead Hurricane Inquiry," *New York Times*, September 20.

PART II
Inside the Politics of Insecurity

Introduction to Part II

To look more closely at the politics of insecurity, we must shift from exploring broad, long-term historical transformations to analyzing specific, well-defined political episodes—that is, from state protection to collective insecurity itself. Only a case study approach will allow us to understand how political leaders participate in the construction of collective insecurity.

To start, Part II formulates a coherent framework adapted to the analysis of specific political episodes during which collective insecurity and state protection become prominent. Chapter Four articulates this framework, emphasizing the crucial role of political leaders in the construction of insecurity. The four remaining chapters compare and contrast distinct political episodes in order to stress common logic and significant variations from one case and policy arena to another. These four cases have been selected in part because they are very different from one another, showing that common logic exists across areas of state protection.[1]

As Part II stresses, political leaders play pivotal roles in the construction of collective insecurity, even when they adopt an essentially reactive role. These actors do not always shape the insecurity agenda, nor do they have absolute control over collective perceptions. Most of the threats these leaders deal with are real, and their capacity to respond to such threats is limited by fiscal and institutional constraints. Taking these limitations into account, Part II explains how the actions and discourse of political leaders truly matter.

---

[1]For a discussion about qualitative sociological comparisons featuring highly contrasted cases, see Dough McAdam, Sidney Tarrow, and Charles Tilly (2001), *Dynamics of Contention* (Cambridge: Cambridge University Press).

Analyzing the Politics of Insecurity

The following chapter sketches an original framework for the study of the politics of insecurity.[1] Dealing with scholarship on "moral panic," the first section suggests that, although useful, this concept applies to only a limited range of episodes; genuine panic episodes are relatively rare. The second section explores the idea of "risk society," revealing the acute risk awareness that characterizes our historical era, and discussing the related concept of organized irresponsibility. Modern political leaders are frequently blamed for events that are not under their control; when a problem occurs, citizens turn to the state and its agents. The third section builds on these topics to explore the strategies political leaders use in developing a politics of insecurity. The fourth section explains how existing policies and political institutions affect such strategies, and the fifth explores the roles of agenda setting and framing processes. This section ends with a discussion of the distinction between proactive and reactive behavior crucial to the understanding of major differences between the four empirical cases analyzed in subsequent chapters.

Moral Panic

The concept of moral panic is a controversial element of contemporary sociological debates on collective insecurity.[2] A moral panic emerges when a "condition, episode, person or group of persons emerges to become defined as a threat to societal values and interests. . . ."[3] Moral entrepreneurs, from politicians to journalists to religious leaders, participate in the social construction of this threat by drawing public attention to it.

Stanley Cohen coined the term "folk devils" to refer to the deviant individuals seen as a direct threat to social order. According to literature on this subject, media reports and the discourse of moral entrepreneurs help transform these characters into a source of collective insecurity. For example, during an episode of moral panic related to an alleged increase in youth delinquency, journalists and politicians may depict urban delinquents as "folk devils." Because these delinquents are seen as a collective threat, repressive measures are proposed to control them. Moral panics like this example have five main characteristics:

> First, there must be a heightened level of *concern* over the behavior of a certain group or category and the consequences that that behavior presumably causes for the rest of society. . . . Second, there must be an increased level of hostility toward the group or category regarded as engaging in the behavior in question. . . . Third, there must be substantial or widespread agreement or consensus . . . that the threat is real, serious and caused by the wrongdoing group members and their behavior. . . . Fourth, there is the implicit assumption . . . the threat . . . is [depicted as] far more substantial [than a realistic evaluation would suggest]. And fifth, by their very nature, moral panics are *volatile*; they erupt fairly suddenly (although they may lie dormant or latent for long periods of time, and may reappear from time to time and, nearly as suddenly, subside).[4]

Drawing on this model, studies about moral panic have explored issues as varied as drug abuse, juvenile delinquency, and flag burning.[5]

Although insightful, the concept of moral panic has major limitations and, as the case studies will suggest, cannot account for major aspects of the politics of insecurity.[6] Stressing the limitations of this concept clarifies some of the assumptions that will guide our analysis of the case studies. First, particular forms of collective insecurity cannot always be directly attributed to a certain group of people. Although it is not hard to blame terrorism or violent crime on "folk devils," it is more difficult to attribute high unemployment or environmental problems like pollution to a particular group or individual. The presence or absence of "folk devils" is related to the threat infrastructure of the policy area at stake: certain threats have a strong moral meaning, while others do not. Moreover, as opposed to man-made threats, many sources of collective insecurity, such as hurricanes and tornadoes, have no explicit moral meaning.

Second, though scholarship on moral panic stresses that threats can be exaggerated, this is certainly not always the case. In fact, politicians often attempt to downplay or even to hide some potential threats from the public, especially when the threat at stake is less known to the public. Chapter Five's analysis of the BSE case will back this claim.

Third, in contrast with cases discussed in scholarship on moral panic, socially constructed forms of insecurity are not always episodic. Some of them—for example, those related to massive unemployment or epidemic diseases like AIDS—can last for years or even decades. The debate over healthcare coverage in the United States, discussed in Chapter Eight, will illustrate this.

Fourth, the idea of panic is itself problematic. Numerous studies have shown that, even when dealing with worst-case disasters, most citizens do not really "panic" at all; genuine panic episodes are rarer than literature on moral panic suggests.[7] Moreover, evidence to prove that a major panic episode has occurred is hard to find; most moral panic studies focus on media accounts, but just because most media outlets focus on dramatic events and sensational news items does not mean that their audience is necessarily frightened or preoccupied by what they hear on the news.[8]

Organized Irresponsibility

German sociologist Ulrich Beck formulated the concept of risk society as a response to the emergence of new environmental hazards related to human activities: "Risk society begins where nature ends. . . . This is where we switch the focus of our anxieties from what nature can do to us to what we have done to nature."[9] Consequently, for Beck, the notion of risk emerges in a world "characterized by the loss of a clear distinction between nature and culture;"[10] environmental issues like pollution and nuclear waste disposal become a major source of anxiety, and safety becomes society's main social and political objective.[11]

Contemporary citizens are acutely aware of environmental risks,[12] and this awareness is politically significant because it leads ordinary citizens to rely increasingly on experts and policymakers to evaluate and fight collective threats. Partly because citizens depend on experts and officials they seldom know personally to fight environmental threats, risk awareness is increasingly related to the issue of trust.[13] The next chapter will show how the state's failure to deal with a specific environmental hazard can undermine public trust.

With risk awareness, "organized irresponsibility"—Beck's idea that it is difficult to identify those responsible for many environmental disasters—directly shapes contemporary politics. "Risks are no longer attributable to external agency. . . . Society becomes a laboratory, but there is no one responsible for its outcomes."[14] Of course, some outcomes *are* easy to trace; we can find out who is behind oil spills or other environmental catastrophes.[15] But beyond this remark, organized irresponsibility is a useful concept because it points to the fact that politicians themselves are "made responsible for decisions they didn't take and for consequences and threats they know nothing about."[16]

This unwarranted blame extends beyond environmental issues. For example, when employers terminate private pension plans, affected workers may call the state for help; if their pleas are not satisfied, these workers may blame politicians for not supporting them with new regulations or relief measures.[17] Considering the expansion of state protection discussed in Part I, elected officials and civil servants deal with an increasing number of economic, social, and environmental issues that can become a source of major political risks for these officials. This leads them to respond by pursuing new political strategies.

Political Strategies

In liberal democracies like Britain, France, and the United States, most politicians pursue at least four goals. First, they seek election and reelection; second, once in office, they try to boost their institutional power within their party or government; third, they attempt to create a positive, enduring political legacy; and fourth, some promote a coherent ideological agenda like neoliberalism or social democracy. If such promotion proves unpopular, it may consequently detract from a politician's attainment of the three other goals. To attain these four goals, political leaders pursue two strategies: credit claiming and blame avoidance.

Credit claiming refers to how politicians take responsibility for "good news," such as the adoption of popular legislation or a decline in crime or unemployment rates.[18] In some instances, a plausible causal relationship exists between a political decision and specific economic or environmental outcomes; for example, a new policy that boosts unemployment benefits is likely to reduce levels of poverty and economic insecurity. But in other cases, the relationship between specific political decisions and concrete economic, social, or environmental outcomes is more tenuous. Thus, elected officials often claim credit for higher economic growth and declining unemployment rates even though the relationship between this "good news" and the policies they promoted is difficult to assess or even impossible to establish. "Good news" and attempts to claim credit for it stimulate debate over who is truly responsible: Is it the current administration, or the previous one? Is the "good news" tied to concrete political decisions? Could the news have been even better if other measures had been enacted? These are the types of questions that emerge in political battles that are rooted in credit-claiming strategies.

Credit claiming is a widely-used strategy, but it is less central to the politics of insecurity than blame avoidance. Blame avoidance generally concerns "bad news," such as terrorist attacks, environmental disasters, and higher unemployment, that may increase collective insecurity. In the logic of organized irresponsibility, elected politicians are frequently blamed for "bad news" even when it is not directly tied to their decisions. Even when other actors like private businesses are believed to be responsible for a negative situation, citizens and journalists may still blame political leaders for their apparent failure to prevent it from occurring or to punish those who are behind it. For example, ordinary citizens and labor leaders may blame downsizing in the private sector on elected officials, despite the problem not being directly linked to any specific political decisions.

Elected officials try to shelter themselves against blame stemming directly from their own policy decisions. Unpopular fiscal measures that seek to balance the budget and restructure state protection also constitute "bad news," as these measures usually call for tax increases and/or cuts in popular programs. As discussed in Chapter Two, since the late 1970s, neoliberal fiscal austerity has increased the political risks elected officials face because these officials may feel compelled to enact unpopular cutbacks in order to balance the budget. Such cutbacks and their potentially negative effect on state protection have become major sources of political blame.[19]

Modern elected officials have developed an array of strategies to prevent, deflect, or delay blame generated by "bad news."[20] For instance, these officials may argue that economic cycles, rather than their past decisions, are responsible for a sudden increase in unemployment. Or in the case of a terrorist attack, those in power may blame their predecessors for a failure to take appropriate measures to fight terrorism. Members of the Bush Administration used this tactic in the aftermath of the September 11, 2001 attacks; in his testimony to the National Commission on Terrorist Attacks on the United States, Attorney General John Ashcroft blamed the Clinton Administration for intelligence faults that may have contributed to the failure to prevent the attacks.[21]

Downplaying the scope of the threats citizens face can also become a political blame avoidance strategy, particularly when the public has limited knowledge of these threats. Stating that debated threats have been exaggerated may justify past and present inaction, in turn shielding elected officials from blame. For instance, an elected official may downplay the effects of global warming in order to avoid blame for the adoption of lax

environmental legislation. Conversely, inflating perceived threats may also deflect blame from political leaders when their opponents depict their policy proposals as too radical. As mentioned in Chapter One, for example, President Bush overdramatized the threat that the Hussein regime posed to American national security to justify the invasion of Iraq.

Institutions, Policies, and Vested Interests

Political strategies are best examined in their specific institutional context. National states and institutions are still at the center of the politics of insecurity in advanced industrial societies, and in these states formal political institutions largely affect the behavior of elected officials and interest groups.[22] The American Congressional system is especially permeable to the direct influence of interest groups:

> In the United States, outside interest groups are able to play an active role in the legislative process because there are so many points of entry into the system—Congress is characterized by decentralization and a detailed division of labor. No one party or member or committee can totally dominate any given issue, and interest groups attempt to influence each of these actors.[23]

Additionally, electoral schedules set the timeframe according to which candidates and elected officials deal with major policy issues. Politicians do not necessarily behave the same way immediately before and after an election; they may propose ambitious reforms during a tight electoral campaign but adopt far more modest measures after the election.

Also, formal political institutions like constitutional frameworks create constraints and opportunities for elected officials and other political leaders, and affect the manner in which these actors claim credit and avoid blame. In the American political system, checks and balances and the lack of strong party discipline in Congress help diffuse blame; in this system, it is often difficult to blame a single actor or party for "bad news" and unpopular legislation. Conversely, in parliamentary countries like Britain and Canada, party discipline and the fusion of legislative and executive power makes it more difficult for members of the ruling party to disperse blame; the party in power is generally seen as responsible for the enactment of unpopular legislation.[24]

Moreover, in the United States, the division of power between Congress and the president is often detrimental to the enactment of bold federal reforms outside episodes of national crisis, partly because without party discipline it is difficult to create winning legislative coalitions. In such a constraining institutional environment, political leaders and interest groups may attempt to create a sense of national crisis to promote the enactment of bold policy initiatives.[25] But a sense of national crisis often stems from concrete, dramatic events that help reshape the political landscape. The Great Depression, the assassination of President John F. Kennedy, and the attacks of September 11, 2001 are among the events that facilitated the enactment of major legislative reforms in the United States.[26]

To elaborate winning electoral and political strategies, political leaders must take into account not only binding rules and institutions, but also existing policies and vested interests. In social policy, large programs often lead to the creation of powerful constituencies, as Social Security led to the creation of the American Association for Retired Persons (AARP). The interests of these constituencies are institutionalized, generally preventing any massive, unilateral attacks against them; an elected official attempting to implement cutbacks in these programs would face major electoral risks.[27]

The emergence of alternative providers of protection and vested interests in the private sector can also generate constraints and opportunities for policymakers.[28] This is clearly the case in the American healthcare sector, where private insurance companies generally oppose national health insurance. However, these perceived interests evolve according to the economic and political context; powerful interest groups that have long opposed key reforms may change their attitudes after a major economic or political shift occurs. For example, Chapter Six discusses how the attacks of September 11, 2001, affected the aviation industry's position on costly airline security measures.

Though vested interests and existing policy arrangements affect all areas of state protection, variations in policy arrangements and vested interests show major political differences from one area of state intervention to another. On one hand, social policies like Social Security that positively affect a large segment of the population create powerful armies of beneficiaries such as the AARP—a situation that generally favors the preservation of such policies. On the other, in the United States at least, broad environmental regulations tend to generate weaker and less-defined constituencies. The positive effects of such regulations are less visible and slower to materialize than are the checks millions of citizens receive from programs like Social Security. Moreover, in the United States and other countries, environmental policies face incessant lobbying from powerful business interests that oppose such regulations.

In addition to existing policies and vested interests, the particular nature of the threat a public policy tackles—its threat infrastructure—explains political variations from one state protection area to another. Spectacular and episodic threats like terrorism stimulate major political decisions more quickly than low-profile hazards that have not yet been publicly defined as major dangers. Threats that attract media attention have a greater chance to stimulate political action than less palpable issues that, in the long run, may actually represent a greater threat to society.[29] Along the same lines, the timeframe that experts and political leaders use for assessing threats also affects the way they react. Smaller scope, shorter-term threats—like a small oil spill near a tourist area, for example—may become more crucial for political leaders seeking reelection than widespread, longer-term issues—like global warming. This situation stems partly from the compact timeframe of modern electoral politics, in which politicians run for re-election every six, four, or even two years.

Another factor that affects policy outcomes is the social and political status of those affected by these threats. For example, in a political system in which money plays a central role, it might be hard for the poor to secure the enactment of comprehensive state protection measures against threats like economic insecurity. The current American situation provides ground to this claim.

Agendas, Frames, and Insecurity

Alongside institutions and vested interests, agenda setting and framing processes are major aspects of the politics of insecurity. The concept of agenda refers to "the list of subjects or problems to which governmental officials, and people outside of government closely associated with those officials, are paying some serious attention at any given time."[30] From this perspective, agenda setting is the social and political process that reduces the "set of conceivable subjects to the set that actually becomes the focus of attention."[31] Experts, journalists, and political leaders participate in the construction of the policy agenda and of the issues that move in and out of it.[32] Since citizens and elected officials cannot focus simultaneously on more than a few key policy issues, the selection of the problems that enter the agenda is crucial to the policy-making process.[33] Consequently, the study of the politics of insecurity must take into consideration beliefs about what the most urgent problems of the day are. For instance, conservative politicians and interest groups may argue that expanding the size of the military is the most pressing issue of the day, while left-leaning actors could think that unemployment and social inequality should take priority.

Ideological frames are discursive interpretations of the world that help shape the way people understand an issue and what should be done about it. Drawing on shared symbols and values, elected officials frame their decisions to avoid blame for "bad news" or claim credit for "good news." For example, a politician could frame illegal immigration as the main source of crime, which would in turn justify a crackdown on that type of immigration. Another example of framing is the argument that helped justify the enactment of the 1996 welfare reform in the United States: welfare supposedly weakens personal responsibility, and therefore the state should limit the amount of time people who are able to work can spend on welfare. Frames like these "appear typically in the public pronouncements of policy makers and their aides, such as sound bites, campaign speeches, press releases, and other statements designed to muster public support for policy proposals."[34] A strategic and deliberate activity, framing concerns the formulation of a discourse that may generate public support for specific actors and proposals.[35]

Ideological frames play a major role in the social construction of collective threats. By framing the perception of threats, political leaders attempt to depict themselves as the best providers of collective protection in order to increase their popular support and to shape a positive, lasting legacy, as the post–September 11, 2001 discourse of President Bush on terrorism demonstrates. Related to blame avoidance and credit claiming strategies, the construction of threats and insecurity through framing processes is at the center of the following analysis of the politics of insecurity.

When constructing collective threats, political leaders can pursue either proactive or reactive behavior. Leaders who adopt proactive behavior attempt directly to draw public attention to a particular source of insecurity. By dramatizing potential threats, these leaders help create conditions for an episode of acute collective insecurity. The case study in Chapter Seven explores the debate over urban delinquency in France by examining proactive behavior on the part of political leaders; in this case, French President Jacques Chirac attempted to shift public attention to the threat of crime, which he claimed to respond to more adequately than his rival Lionel Jospin.

Political leaders who engage in reactive behavior attempt to reframe to their advantage a major episode of collective insecurity that emerged independent of their actions. While these leaders are not responsible for putting a threat on the agenda, they are involved in the shaping of threat perception. During the 1996 BSE episode, for example, British Prime Minister John Major did his best to divert attention from his party's policy record by mobilizing nationalist rhetoric in defense of British beef.

Beyond the distinction between proactive and reactive behavior, we should always keep in mind that political leaders are not the only actors involved in framing struggles. Regularly, divergent voices from civil society may criticize dominant frames before challenging the explanations those in power formulate. In liberal democracies, skeptical citizens and journalists may mobilize to question sanctioned stories and to force officials to provide new accounts.[36] This happened in the United States of the late 1960s, when grassroots opposition to the Vietnam War gained strength and questioned the official rationale for war.

This chapter sketched a unified framework for the analysis of the politics of insecurity, isolating five major claims that will guide the following comparative analysis. First, although illuminating, the concept of moral panic applies to only a limited range of insecurity episodes. Genuine panic episodes are relatively rare, and they do not necessarily involve scapegoats or clearly defined moral issues. Second, citizens of advanced industrial societies exhibit acute risk awareness. When new collective threats emerge, the logic of collective irresponsibility leads citizens and interest groups alike to blame political leaders or, at least, to turn to the state for protection. Third, political leaders mobilize credit claiming and blame avoidance strategies to respond to—and frame—these threats in a way that enhances their political position. Fourth, powerful interests and institutional forces, as well as the threat infrastructure specific to a policy area, create constraints and opportunities for political actors. Finally, the behavior of political leaders is either proactive or reactive, as they can push a threat onto the agenda or attempt to shape perceptions of this threat after other forces have transformed it into a major political issue.

The discussions from this chapter guide the subsequent case studies, which illustrate the major role of political leaders in the construction of collective insecurity and state protection. These four cases also emphasize the specificity of each episode, its threat infrastructure, and contingent events that shape the politics of insecurity.

Notes

1. This chapter draws on Daniel Béland (2007), "Insecurity and Politics: A Framework," *Canadian Journal of Sociology* 32(3).
2. In 1971, British sociologist Jock Young made the first published reference to moral panic in a book chapter on drug abuse and policing in Britain; see Young, "The Role of the Police as Amplifiers of Deviance: Negotiators of Drug Control as Seen in Notting Hill" in Stanley Cohen, ed., *Images of Deviance* (Harmondsworth: Penguin).

For a history of the concept of moral panic, see Kenneth Thompson (1998), *Moral Panics* (London: Routledge), p. 7; or Chas Critcher (2003), *Moral Panics and the Media* (Buckingham: Open University Press), pp. 9–30.

3. Stanley Cohen (1972), *Folk Devils and Moral Panics: The Creation of the Mods and Rockers* (Oxford: Blackwell), p. 28.

4. Erich Goode and Nachman Ben-Yehuda (1994), *Moral Panics* (Oxford: Blackwell), pp. 33–38.

5. See, for example, Philip Jenkins (1992), *Intimate Enemies: Moral Panics in Contemporary Great Britain* (New York: Aldine de Gruyter), and Michael Welch (2000), *Flag Burning: Moral Panic and the Criminalization of Protest* (New York: Aldine de Gruyter).

6. For a critical discussion on moral panic, see Goode and Ben-Yehuda, *Moral Panics: The Social Construction of Deviance*; Sean P. Hier (2003), "Risk and Panic in Late Modernity: Implications of the Converging Sites of Social Anxiety," *British Journal of Sociology* 54(1): 3–20 (4); and Angela McRobbie and Sarah L. Thornton (1995), "Rethinking 'Moral Panic' for Multi-Mediated Social Worlds," *British Journal of Sociology* 46(4): 559–74.

This chapter's critique of moral panic draws from Sheldon Ungar's excellent 2001 article "Moral Panic versus Risk Society: The Implications of the Changing Sites of Social Anxiety," *British Journal of Sociology* 52(2): 271–91.

7. For a critique of the concept of panic, see Lee Clarke (2006), *Worst Cases: Terror and Catastrophe in the Popular Imagination* (Chicago: University of Chicago Press), pp. 109–11.

8. Ungar, "Moral Panic versus Risk Society," p. 279.

9. Ulrich Beck (1998), "The Politics of Risk Society," in Jane Franklin, ed., *The Politics of Risk Society* (Cambridge: Polity Press), pp. 9–22.

10. Ibid.

11. Beck (1986, rpt. 1992), *Risk Society* (London: Sage Publications).

For a discussion of the risk society thesis, see Barbara Adam, Ulrich Beck, and Joost van Loon, eds. (2000), *The Risk Society and Beyond: Critical Issues for Social Theory* (London: Sage Publications).

12. Michael D. Mehta (1997), "Re-Licensing of Nuclear Facilities in Canada: The 'Risk Society' in Action," *Electronic Journal of Sociology* 3(1) (available online at www.sociology.org/content/vol003.001/mehta.html [accessed March 2007]).

13. Anthony Giddens (1990), *The Consequences of Modernity* (Stanford, CA: Stanford University Press).

14. Beck, "The Politics of Risk Society," p. 14.

15. On the link between responsibility claims and environmental disasters, see Thomas A. Birkland (1997), *After Disaster: Agenda Setting,*

Public Policy and Focusing Events (Washington, DC: Georgetown University Press).

16. Beck, "The Politics of Risk Society," p. 14.

17. See, for example, Jim Abrams (2005), "Senate Passes Bill to Shore up Pensions," *Washington Post*, November 16 (available online at www.washingtonpost.com/wp-dyn/content/article/2005/12/15/AR2005121502031.html [accessed March 2007]).

18. For a classic analysis of credit-claiming strategies in the American Congress, see David R. Mayhew (1974), *Congress: The Electoral Connection* (New Haven, CT: Yale University Press).

19. Paul Pierson (1994), *Dismantling the Welfare State? Reagan, Thatcher and the Politics of Retrenchment* (Cambridge: Cambridge University Press).

20. R. Kent Weaver (1986), "The Politics of Blame Avoidance," *Journal of Public Policy* 6 (October–December): 371–98.
    For an application of the concept of blame avoidance to the politics of insecurity, see Sean P. Hier (2002), "Raves, Risks and the Ecstasy Panic: A Case Study in the Subversive Nature of Moral Regulation," *Canadian Journal of Sociology* 27(1): 33–57.

21. Adam Nagourney and Eric Lichtblau (2004), "Evaluating the 9/11 Hearings' Winners and Losers," *New York Times*, April 18.

22. See André Lecours, ed. (2005), *New Institutionalism: Theory and Analysis* (Toronto: University of Toronto Press); Sven Steinmo, Kathleen Thelen, and Frank Longstreth, eds. (1992), *Structuring Politics: Historical Institutionalism in Comparative Analysis* (New York: Cambridge University Press); and R. Kent Weaver and Bert Rockman, eds. (1993), *Do Institutions Matter? Government Capabilities in the U.S. and Abroad* (Washington, DC: Brookings Institution).

23. Norman Ornstein (1998), *The Role of the Legislature in a Democracy*, Freedom Paper No. 3 (Washington, DC: U.S. Department of State; available online at usinfo.state.gov/products/pubs/archive/freedom/freedom3.htm [accessed March 2007]).

24. Paul Pierson and R. Kent Weaver (1993), "Imposing Losses in Pension Policy," in R. Kent Weaver and Bert A. Rockman, eds., *Do Institutions Matter? Government Capabilities in the United States and Abroad* (Washington, DC: Brookings Institution), pp. 110–50.

25. The author would like to thank John Myles for his insight on this issue.

26. From the Great Depression came the New Deal; from the Democratic landslide following the assassination of President Kennedy came Medicare and the War on Poverty; and from September 11, 2001 came measures dealing with national security such as the Patriot Act.

27. Pierson, *Dismantling the Welfare State?*

28. Jacob S. Hacker (2002), *The Divided Welfare State: The Battle over Public and Private Social Benefits in the United States* (Cambridge: Cambridge University Press).

29. In literature on risk perception and communication, "risk amplification" describes the process by which hazards that are low in risk can become the focus of social and political attention. Recent examples of "risk amplification" include BSE and plane crashes.

    For more on this, see Jeanne X. Kasperson, Roger E. Kasperson, Nick Pidgeon, and Paul Slovic (2003), "The Social Amplification of Risk: Assessing Fifteen Years of Research and Theory," in Nick Pidgeon, Roger E. Kasperson, and Paul Slovic, eds., *The Social Amplification of Risk* (Cambridge: Cambridge University Press), pp. 13–46.

    On risk perception and communication, see Paul Slovic (2000), *The Perception of Risk* (London: Earthscan).

30. John W. Kingdon (1995), *Agendas, Alternatives, and Public Policies*, Second Edition (New York: HarperCollins), p. 3.

    On agenda setting, see Frank R. Baumgartner and Bryan D. Jones (1993), *Agendas and Instability in American Politics* (Chicago: University of Chicago Press).

31. Kingdon, *Agendas, Alternatives, and Public Policies*, p. 3.

32. Daniel Béland (2005), "Ideas and Social Policy: An Institutionalist Perspective," *Social Policy and Administration* 39(1): 1–18.

33. On the social and political construction of policy problems, see David A. Rochefort and Roger W. Cobb, eds. (1994), *The Politics of Problem Definition* (Lawrence: University Press of Kansas).

    Dramatic events like environmental disasters can have a strong impact on policy agendas; see Birkland, *After Disaster*.

34. John L. Campbell (1998), "Institutional Analysis and the Role of Ideas in Political Economy," *Theory and Society* 27: 377–409.

    On the political role of frames and discourse, see Mark Blyth (2002), *Great Transformations: Economic Ideas and Institutional Change in the Twentieth Century* (Cambridge: Cambridge University Press); Murray Edelman (1988), *Constructing the Political Spectacle* (Chicago: University of Chicago Press), pp. 697–712; and Vivien A. Schmidt (2002), *The Futures of European Capitalism* (Oxford: Oxford University Press).

35. Robert H. Cox (2001), "The Social Construction of an Imperative: Why Welfare Reform Happened in Denmark and the Netherlands but Not in Germany," *World Politics* 53: 463–98.

36. Charles Tilly (2006), *Why?* (Princeton: Princeton University Press), p. 174.

Mad Cow Politics

Though awareness of food safety has always existed, modern citizens are increasingly aware of food hazards caused by pollution, mishandling, and technological change.[1] The modern state has set regulations and control mechanisms to reduce the scope of food-related health hazards, including microbial contamination such as salmonella, pesticide residues, and environmental contaminants such as mercury. In recent years, the food safety debate has expanded to include controversial technological innovations like genetically modified crops and the injection of carbon monoxide into meat to make it look fresher. In addition, the increasing global exchange of the food supply has intensified safety concerns. While relatively expensive to run, regulation programs are important because they maintain or restore popular confidence in the food industry.

Among contemporary food hazards, Bovine Spongiform Encephalopathy (BSE, or "mad cow disease") is perhaps best known. Public awareness of BSE in the 1980s and 1990s spread quickly for three reasons: first, the term "mad cow disease" conjures concrete images of terror; second, BSE concerns a meat widely consumed in Western societies; and third, citizens cannot directly detect the disease in the meat they buy. A potential source of sudden episodes of insecurity, the disease has been found in an increasing number of countries over the last two decades, during which the expansion of international trade has aggravated fears of global propagation.

This chapter studies the first major political debate over BSE: the spectacular 1996 British BSE episode. The discussion will show how scientific research on BSE became intrinsically political and how British officials downplayed the potential public health hazards related to BSE.[2] We will also see how this situation illustrated tactics of credit claiming and blame avoidance: after finally admitting the existence of public health risks, the British Conservative government of John Major quickly shifted public attention to the European ban on British beef. British nationalism thus became a blame avoidance strategy during this episode.

The Nature and Perceived Origin
of the Threat

BSE belongs to a group of animal diseases, Transmissible Spongiform Encephalopathies (TSEs), that have long occurred in mammalian species:

> The form of the disease in sheep is called scrapie, and it has been present in
> Britain and in several other countries for well over 200 years. The form of
> the disease in humans is called Creutzfeldt-Jakob Disease (CJD) and it has
> also been known for a long time.[3]

Both BSE and CJD are chronic, degenerative diseases that affect the central nervous system of the infected animal or person. Although some cattle had probably been infected with BSE during the 1970s, British scientists recorded the first cases in spring 1985; it took them nearly two more
years to identify the new disease.

In late October 1987, scientists from the Central Veterinary Laboratory
published an article that alerted the British scientific community to BSE.[4]
After this, scientists debated the causal link between BSE and CJD. Such a
link would mean that consuming infected meat could lead to CJD, thus
making BSE not only an animal disease but also a major public health issue. Strong evidence now shows that BSE causes CJD, but no consensus
on this issue could be reached in the mid-1980s. Limited scientific and
public knowledge allowed British civil servants and Conservative political
leaders to preclude the public from viewing the BSE outbreak as a potential public health hazard, thereby avoiding blame for past policy decisions
and protecting the short-term vested interests of the national beef industry. Scientific research on BSE became a significant political issue in the
1980s, and the British state attempted to shape the scientific research
agenda through its funding policies.

Two broad contextual factors may have favored the emergence and the
spread of BSE during the 1980s. Although the first of these, industrial and
technological change, is not directly related to public policies and regulations, the second, neoliberal economic deregulation, had a strong political meaning that created electoral risks for the Conservative governments
of Margaret Thatcher (1979–1990) and John Major (1990–1997).

Significant changes in the British rendering industry in the early 1980s
affected both its production processes and organizational structure. "The
industry was becoming geographically concentrated in large scale plants
and subject to strong pressures toward monopoly ownership."[5] Related to
this, the industry introduced a new energy-saving rendering process that

reduced operative temperatures to a range of only 80–90 degrees—against the previous 130—without sterilization processes required in other countries and despite MAFF (Ministry of Agriculture, Food and Fisheries) research showing the need for high temperature processes to kill the scrapie agent in wasted sheep meat and subsequently published warnings of the associated dangers.[6]

Some observers argued that such changes in the rendering of sheep and cattle remains, as well as the transformation of some of these remains into high-protein feed for cattle, favored the propagation of BSE in Britain. However, the official BSE inquiry launched in 1996 rejected this claim.[7]

Before the discovery of BSE, little was done to regulate the British rendering industry. But as early as 1979, a Royal Commission on Environmental Pollution recommended that "the feeding of rendered animal remains to ruminants be banned."[8] Committed to neoliberalism and economic deregulation, the incoming Conservative government of Margaret Thatcher rejected that recommendation, instead enacting legislation in 1981 that established self-regulation in the rendering industry. This neoliberal approach loosened the British food safety regime.

Though it is impossible to establish a direct causal link between deregulation and the advent of BSE, the disease's emergence only a few years after the election of the Conservative government created electoral risks for the ruling party and its supporters. Because of the high power concentration in the British parliamentary system, it was difficult for the ruling party to escape blame generated by controversial policy decisions.[9] Critics established an apparent link between deregulation and BSE, meaning that the Thatcher government faced blame for the spreading of an animal disease still unknown when the Conservative Party took office in 1979. This apparent link increased political incentives for Conservatives to downplay potential public health hazards associated with BSE.

During the 1980s and 1990s, the legacies of deregulation had two other consequences for BSE politics. First, deregulation increased the policy influence of market imperatives like profitability, which mattered most for the meat industry. Second, "changes in the funding arrangements for the research councils and for scientific research institutes . . . meant that the market [had] a greater role in determining research rather than the priorities of either public policy or scientific progress."[10] As research institutes became mere business organizations, commercial funding increased the dependency of researchers on private interests like the meat industry itself. The strengthening of the implicit alliance between the agricultural sector and the MAFF led to the reinforcement of private, vested economic interests in the fields of risk evaluation and food safety. As suggested below, the agenda of the meat industry increasingly affected the MAFF's own agenda.

How Bureaucratic Agencies Downplayed the Threat

In the years following the discovery of BSE, some British scientists suggested that this animal disease, if ingested, may cause CJD in humans, thus representing a potential public health hazard:[11]

> In 1988, British Professor R. Lacey had pointed out the danger of the disease in cows. He also suggested that the disease could possibly be transmitted to humans. At the time, however, he had no definitive proof to support his claim. Even though his view was shared by several scientists, the UK government did not realize the magnitude of the reports and instead perpetuated a message that British beef was safe to eat.[12]

Thus, during the second half of the 1980s, the official discourse of British civil servants framed BSE as an exclusively animal health issue, not a public health issue. Reassuring discourse on the absence of a public health threat stemming from BSE served the short-term interests of the meat industry, which attempted to maintain public confidence in British beef in Britain and abroad. The initial definition of BSE as an animal health issue had lasting political consequences; the "no human risk" rhetoric of British officials later lost credibility in the context of increasingly alarming media and scientific reports.[13]

Among state agencies dealing with BSE and other food safety issues, the MAFF is probably the most influential. Related to powerful interest groups like the National Farmers' Union, the MAFF pursues two potentially contradictory policy goals. On one hand, it promotes British agriculture and its products at home and abroad, defending the immediate interests of the private agricultural sector within and outside the British state. On the other hand, the MAFF is directly involved in quality control and food safety through many of its expert committees, agencies, and study groups. Because the MAFF is related to farming and rendering industries, its capacity to protect consumers against food-related threats is problematic.

MAFF's initial attitude after the discovery of BSE was similar to their reaction to other food scares of that time, such as the *Salmonella* outbreaks of the late 1980s and the increase in illness due to *Listeria* in the 1970s and 1980s.

> In each case MAFF's approach was initial denial followed by a reluctant admission of minimal risk until forced to acknowledge a degree of serious risk in the face of overwhelming evidence and public disbelief in its stance.[14]

After the identification of BSE, the MAFF promoted the idea that BSE could not affect human health in any significant way.[15] Three joint committees

established by MAFF and the Department of Health provided the scientific evidence at the foundation of this discourse. As stated, the link between BSE and CJD had not been clearly established by the late 1980s, but rather than adopting a precautionary approach—playing safe when facing uncertainty—the MAFF adopted a proportional approach—regulating no more than needed according to the scientific evidence available. MAFF thus justified a modest policy response to BSE coherent with the short-term interests of the beef industry.[16]

Furthermore, evidence shows that through their funding policy, the MAFF and other state agencies attempted to shape scientific research on BSE. For example:

> some MAFF researchers have been prevailed upon to direct their enquiries into areas which were likely to support the official line of risk to humans. . . . Furthermore, when research was carried out, MAFF has intervened to alter official reports and the contents of papers in scientific journals.[17]

And after the *British Medical Journal* published evidence that BSE was a potential public health concern, a MAFF-sponsored commission assessed such a threat as "remote."[18]

Illustrating the political significance of scientific research in advanced industrial societies, this attempt to control the research agenda was related to a broader framing strategy aimed at shaping the public's perception of BSE. For the MAFF as well as the meat industry, reassuring the public at home and abroad about the safety of British beef was crucial. Negating any potential public health hazard stemming from BSE seemed necessary in order to maintain the public's trust in British beef; without this trust, beef sales at home would decline and foreign states would impose a ban on British meat that could damage the industry. At the time, the politics of insecurity thus involved framing the issue in a manner that negated any potential threat to human health, constraining scientific research and framing available information. While there is no evidence that British officials knew that BSE constituted a serious public health hazard, the MAFF did attempt to restrict the policy agenda by framing BSE as a non–public health issue.

However, the official negation of any potential public health concern did not result in complete policy inaction by MAFF and other state agencies. By June 21, 1988, the number of confirmed BSE cases in the UK had already reached 867, and the number was increasing rapidly.[19] Probably because of this, in the summer of 1988, the British state implemented some measures to fight the disease, including compulsory notification of BSE to the state, the slaughter of suspected infected cattle, and a ban on the use of protein in ruminant feed. These measures were "largely predicated on the assumption that BSE was unlikely to pose a human health risk but that nevertheless the uncertainty required that some precautions be taken."[20] In November 1989, the multiplication of BSE cases in Britain led to more new measures, including regulations on cattle carcass disposal and the consumption of milk from infected cows.

However, these measures proved modest and the early decision to compensate farmers for only 50 percent of the slaughtered animal's value did not provide them with a strong incentive to report BSE cases.[21]

Media and Political Responses

Between 1988 and 1996, BSE became a widely-debated public issue only twice. The British media first addressed BSE as a major topic in May 1990, when scientific research made it clear that "Transmissible Spongiform Encephalopathies (TSEs) could jump the species barrier."[22] The infection of a cat named Max gave the public a symbol for its BSE concerns. Despite the new evidence, the Conservative government denied that BSE represented a significant public health concern. To back the official message that British beef was safe with a powerful, reassuring image, Agriculture Minister John Selwyn Gummer even fed his young daughter Cordelia a 100-percent British beef hamburger in front of television cameras.[23] For members of the Conservative cabinet, eating British beef in public represented a patriotic gesture, a defense of the British beef industry, and more generally a statement about food safety in Britain. Elected officials played active roles in this politics of insecurity.

On June 8, 1990, the European Commission enacted a measure on beef certification for BSE-free herds. Thus, after a few days of widespread exposure, the BSE issue moved to the periphery of the British policy agenda. This illustrates the cyclical nature of media coverage, which shifts rapidly from one prominent issue to another. Public health was probably no more at risk in June 1990 than during preceding months, but the British media ran with this sensational story while it had the public's interest. The media just as quickly lost interest in an issue whose novelty had rapidly declined.

In late 1995, an increasing number of CJD cases led to the resurgence of media interest in BSE. This peaked in March 1996, when British officials acknowledged for the first time that BSE could cause CJD in humans. The sense of uncertainty prevailing at the time pushed the Conservative government to recognize BSE as a major public health issue, and the human health interests of this potential epidemic became dominant for the first time.[24] Representatives of the Labour party challenged Conservative officials to disclose to the public all scientific evidence on BSE. In the House of Commons, Member of Parliament Harriet Harman stated Labour's position on this issue:

> Does the Secretary of State acknowledge that public confidence on this issue is hanging by a thread? Public confidence must be restored, but the public has to be given the full facts and honest advice on which to base their decisions. That relies on two things. It relies, does it not, on the Secretary of State giving full disclosure of the scientific evidence? I hope that he will publish all that information and give clear advice and guidance.[25]

Far from downplaying potential public health hazards, the Conservative government adopted a discourse of crisis. After denying the threat for more than a decade, the Conservative government finally acknowledged it with force, proclaiming that bold actions were necessary to protect both consumers and the British beef industry. According to British scholar Ian Forbes, "the inaccurate estimate of extremely low risk [was] replaced by a new officially sanctioned but equally unsubstantiated account of a much higher risk."[26] The Conservative government faced Labour Party criticism for their legacy of deregulation and the government's unwillingness to acknowledge the public health hazards of BSE. They responded by employing a helpful blame avoidance strategy, claiming that the government had only recently discovered the problem, and emphasizing new evidence of public health hazards. This way, the Conservative government could stress its bold commitment to food safety while maintaining that its members had only recently learned of the public health concerns of BSE.

The British media played an instrumental role in creating an atmosphere of collective insecurity while transforming BSE into a major policy item. On March 20, 1996, for example, the *Daily Mirror* front page exclaimed MAD COW CAN KILL YOU. On that day, Health Secretary Stephen Dorrell admitted in the House of Commons that ten cases of a new strain of CJD could be related to the spread of BSE in cattle since the late 1980s.[27] Over the next few days, the British press focused on the public health insecurity associated with BSE, depicting the disease in spectacular terms as indestructible and extremely dangerous, greatly increasing public insecurity over food hazards.[28] Considering the number of people who actually died from CJD—139 from 1995 through 2003—media reports proved excessively pessimistic.[29]

How did this media mania spread so quickly? As noted in Chapter Two, the threat infrastructure of food safety issues favors sudden episodes of collective insecurity: the threat is both invisible and widespread because of the food's popularity. Second, though BSE is a potential source of insecurity, it is not a moral issue involving genuine "folk devils." This aspect of the BSE threat infrastructure explains why the 1996 episode goes beyond "moral panic." Indeed, the BSE threat caused little widespread or sustained public panic, despite the media hype, partially because those who feared contracting CJD could protect themselves by simply avoiding to eat beef.

On March 27, 1996, several European countries and the European Union imposed a ban on British beef, and the economic situation of the British beef industry quickly became as much a media issue as the public health crisis. The country's economy was under attack: "As the crisis developed all five tabloid newspapers began to focus on the threat posed to the British beef industry from the European ban at the expense of the food health aspects."[30] The campaign against BSE thus took on a strong nationalistic meaning in Britain. On March 21, for example, Prime Minister John Major spoke in Parliament to condemn the European attempt to impose a ban on British beef:

> Important national interests for Britain are involved in this matter. I cannot tolerate those interests being brushed aside by some of our European partners, with no reasonable grounds to do so. The top priority of our European policy must be to get the unjustified ban on beef derivatives lifted as soon as possible and to establish a clear path for the lifting of other aspects of the wider ban. We shall continue our present efforts, although these are not enough.[31]

For the Conservative government, nationalistic rhetoric surrounding the crusade to save the British beef industry constituted an opportunity to shift the public's attention toward the supposedly unfair and irrational behavior of other European countries. Framing the defense of British beef as a nationalist crusade became a reactive blame avoidance strategy for the Conservative government. For example, Conservatives charged Harriet Harman with "talking down British beef" when she accused Conservative cabinet ministers of "reckless disregard for public health" and blamed the "dogma of deregulation for having swept the country into the crisis."[32] Although critical of the government's deregulation and risk communication policies, Labour opposition could only engage in the same nationalistic rhetoric and join Prime Minister Major in his crusade against the European ban. Tony Blair, for one, chimed in:

> We share the great disappointment at the failure to get the ban at least partially lifted. We believe that there is no justification whatever for its continuing. The right regulations are now in place, and all reasonable scientific measures have been taken. Of course we shall support the Government in any sensible moves to ensure that the negotiations are successful.[33]

The nationalistic defense of British beef undermined the opposition's capacity to criticize the Conservative government on its BSE record and past policy decisions. The politics of economic nationalism—i.e., the defense of the British beef industry—took precedence over the politics of insecurity.

Media coverage and global trade pressures made the BSE problem impossible for the Conservative government to avoid. The government, probably as concerned for the future of the British beef industry as with public health, had enacted modest new measures during the first half of the 1990s to restore public confidence in the safety of British beef, including an extension of the ruminant feed ban.[34] After March 20, 1996, however, growing concerns about public health and the European ban on British beef forced the Conservative government to take further action to save a major national industry. On March 28, for example, the government introduced new control measures as well as a massive cattle slaughter program, which came with financial aid to the rendering industry.

As mentioned in Chapter Two, the BSE episode of 1996 forced both British and EU officials to look for better ways to deal with food-related hazards, transcending national borders. In London, as in Brussels, official inquiries were launched in order to draw lessons from the BSE episode while implementing new control and inspection mechanisms. The subsequent creation of the European Food Safety Agency (EFSA) represented a significant step in the institution of a transnational mode of regulation.[35] Because BSE has since been detected in other European countries and elsewhere around the world, food safety is more than ever viewed as a global problem that requires international cooperation.[36]

The recent discovery of BSE-infected cattle in Canada has increased concerns about this disease, and new regulations and surveillance mechanisms have been enacted in Canada and the United States to fight its spread. As in Britain, the Canadian beef industry has been hit by international bans, and nationalistic discourse has emerged in protest. In both countries, elected officials found it convenient to blame other countries for the problem that undermined a significant sector of their national economy. Likewise, Canadian authorities have been reluctant to acknowledge the public health hazards related to BSE, and the Canadian state has implemented measures viewed by many critics as far too modest.[37] As in Britain in the early 1990s, short-term economic interests may have prevailed over a long-term strategy that could improve trust in the food supply and in the state.

Globalization and international trade have played enormous and increasing roles in both the British and Canadian BSE episodes. In both, foreign countries closed their borders to British and Canadian beef in the name of food safety and a strong vision of state protection. Though such decisions favor the emergence of international regulations to ease potential trade conflicts related to a purely national and uncoordinated model of protection, the BSE crises have reinforced the state's protective role in the face of globalizing food hazards. That said, it is the increasingly global nature of the food supply that reinforced traditional demands for state protection in that policy area. Globalization—in this case, the increasingly global nature of the food supply—can have a significant impact on the politics of insecurity and the development of state protection.

Discussion

The British BSE debate of March 1996 illustrates the complexities of the politics of insecurity. Despite growing evidence on the transmission of BSE to human beings, British officials first attempted to shape the scientific research agenda while sending a "no-risk" message to the public. After years of denying or avoiding the public health concerns of BSE, the Conservative government finally became involved in a food insecurity episode that may have not occurred so suddenly had the *potential* threat been communicated to the population earlier.

This chapter has stressed the political role of scientific research and media reports in the construction of collective insecurity. Lack of transparency in risk management may increase the level of concern once the potential threat is finally revealed to the public via media coverage. This situation undermined trust in the British state.[38]

In reviewing the British BSE case, one can revisit the five claims formulated at the end of Chapter Four. First, this case stresses the limitations of the concept of moral panic; the British BSE episode cannot be characterized this way, in part because it involves no "folk devils." Furthermore, this episode was hardly a source of widespread and sustained panic.[39] Second, citizens showed increased risk awareness regarding food safety issues, and held their politicians accountable for past decisions, in this case, industry deregulation. Third, British conservatives attempted to avoid blame, successfully deflecting attention to the foreign nations that instigated a ban on British beef. Fourth, the powerful vested economic interests of the beef industry created constraints for British policymakers, who took these interests into account during all stages of the BSE story.

Finally, this case illustrates the contrast between proactive and reactive strategies in the politics of insecurity. Before 1996, British officials actively shaped the dominant perception that BSE did not constitute a public health hazard. In 1996, however, media-induced food insecurity put the Conservative government in a reactive situation, as it attempted to shift attention from its perceived responsibility for the episode. We see from this that political leaders do not always control the agenda and must enter insecurity debates initiated by other actors—in this case, the British media and, to a lesser extent, Labour opposition. International trade became central to the debate over BSE, and the reactive blame avoidance strategy British conservatives used was related to economic globalization.

Notes

1. See R. C. Dawson, J. M. Cox, A. Almond, and A. Moses (2001), *Food Safety Risk Management in Different Egg Production Systems* (Melbourne: Rural Industries Research and Development Corporation).
2. For an alternative account of the BSE story, see the recollections of Richard Packer, a former British official, in his 2006 book *The Politics of BSE* (Houndmills: Palgrave).
3. Richard W. Lacey (1994), *Mad Cow Disease: The History of BSE in Britain* (St. Helier, Jersey: Cypsela), p. 1.
4. Gerald A. Wells, et al. (1987), "A Novel Progressive Spongiform Encephalopathy in Cattle," *Veterinary Record* 121(18), October 31, pp. 419–20.

    See also Maxime Schwartz (2003), *How the Cows Turned Mad* (Berkeley: University of California Press), p. 143. On the early years of the spreading of BSE, see Lord Phillips of Worth Matravers (2000), *The Inquiry into BSE and Variant CJD in the United Kingdom*, vol. 3 (London: Stationery Office; available online at www.bseinquiry.gov.uk/report/index.htm [accessed March 2007]).
5. David M. C. Bartlett (1999), "Mad Cows and Democratic Governance: BSE and the Construction of a 'Free Market' in the UK," *Crime, Law and Social Change* 30: 237–57.
6. Ibid.
7. Lord Phillips, *The Inquiry into BSE and Variant CJD*.
8. Bartlett, "Mad Cows and Democratic Governance," p. 237.
9. On this issue, see Paul Pierson and R. Kent Weaver (1993), "Imposing Losses in Pension Policy," in R. Kent Weaver and Bert A. Rockman, eds., *Do Institutions Matter? Government Capabilities in the United States and Abroad* (Washington, DC: Brookings Institution), pp. 110–50.
10. David Miller (1999), "Risk, Science and Policy: Definitional Struggles, Information Management, the Media and BSE," *Social Science & Medicine* 49(9): 1239–55 (available online at homepages.strath.ac.uk/~his04105/publications/riskscienceand%20policy.pdf [accessed March 2007]).

11. For a personal account, see Lacey, *Mad Cow Disease*.
12. Catherine Goethals, Scott C. Ratzan, and Veronica Demko (1998), "The Politics of BSE: Negotiating the Public's Health," in Scott C. Ratzan, ed., *The Mad Cow Crisis: Health and the Public Good* (New York: New York University Press), pp. 95–110.
13. See Douglas Powell and William Leiss (1997), *Mad Cows and Mother's Milk: The Perils of Poor Risk Communication* (Montreal: McGill-Queen's University Press), p. 7.
14. Bartlett, "Mad Cows and Democratic Governance," p. 239.
15. Alan Greer (1999), "Policy Coordination and the British Administrative System: Evidence from the BSE Inquiry," *Parliamentary Affairs*, 52(4): 598–633.
16. Martin J. Smith (2004), "Mad Cow and Mad Money: Problems of Risk in the Making and Understanding of Policy," *British Journal of Political Science and International Relations* 6: 312–32.
17. Miller, "Risk, Science and Policy," p. 1245.
18. Bartlett, "Mad Cows and Democratic Governance," p. 240.
19. Lacey (1994), *Mad Cow Disease*, p. 62.
20. Greer, "Policy Coordination and the British Administrative System," p. 601.
21. Ibid. The compensation was later increased to 100 percent.
22. Miller, "Risk, Science and Policy," p. 1247.
23. A video of the BBC's broadcast of this episode is available at news.bbc.co.uk/hi/english/static/special_report/1999/06/99/bse_inquiry/default.stm (accessed March 2007).
24. Miller, "Risk, Science and Policy," p. 1248.
25. Harriet Harman (1996), Commons Hansard Debates, London, March 20, Column 376.
26. Forbes (2004), "Making a Crisis out of a Drama: The Political Analysis of BSE Policy-Making in the UK," *Political Studies* 52: 342–57.
27. Rod Brookes (1999), "Newspapers and National Identity: the BSE/CJD Crisis and the British Press," *Media, Culture and Society* 21(2): 247–263 (250).
28. A. P. Smith, J. A. Young and J. Gibson (1997), "Consumer Information and BSE: Credibility and Edibility" *Risk Decision and Policy* 2(1): 41–51.
29. Between 1995 and 2003, CJD claimed 139 lives in the United Kingdom—an average of eighteen victims a year. See John Innes (2004), "Deaths from CJD up to 18 in 2003," *The Scotsman*, March 2 (available online at news.scotsman.com/topics.cfm?tid=671&id=244672004 [accessed March 2007]).
30. Brookes, "Newspapers and National Identity," p. 251.

31. Prime Minister John Major (1996), Commons Hansard Debates, London, Thursday, March 21, Column 99.
32. Patrick Wintour, Owen Bowcott, and Stephen Bates (1996), "Ministers Defy Beef Outcry," *Guardian*, March 26: 1.
33. Tony Blair (1996), Commons Hansard Debates, London, Thursday, March 21, Column 101.
34. Greer, "Policy Coordination and the British Administrative System," p. 601.
35. Keith Vincent (2004), " 'Mad Cows' and Eurocrats—Community Responses to the BSE Crisis," *European Law Journal*, 10(5): 499–517.
36. The idea that BSE has become a global problem may serve as a blame avoidance strategy for elected officials and civil servants who seek to hide mistakes in their handling of a BSE outbreak. Arguing that a problem exists in other countries may help national political leaders deflect the blame they face.
37. On the recent Canadian debate on BSE, see Douglas Powell and William Leiss (2004), *Mad Cows and Mother's Milk: The Perils of Poor Risk Communication*, Second Edition (Montreal-Kingston: McGill-Queens University Press).
38. In the recent debate on genetically modified organisms (GMOs), many citizens could not believe what their government depicted as scientific evidence. See Erik Millstone and Patrick van Zwanenberg (2000), "A Crisis of Trust: For Science, Scientists or for Institutions?" *Nature Medicine* 6(12), December: 1307–08 (available online at www.nature.com/nm/journal/v6/n12/full/nm1200_1307.html [accessed March 2007]).
39. This did occur: beef consumption in Britain fell by 8 percent in 1996, despite the campaign to support the domestic beef industry. See Foreign Agricultural Service (1998). *The Continuing Effects of BSE Beef Market, Trade, and Policy* (Washington, DC: United States Department of Agriculture; available online at www.fas.usda.gov/dlp2/circular/1998/98-03LP/bse.html [accessed March 2007]).

From Aviation Safety to Security

In the United States and around the world, the events of September 11, 2001, altered how citizens and political leaders view both national security and transportation security. This chapter explores the issue of aviation security in the United States before and after that pivotal day.

International organizations like the International Civil Aviation Organization have long played a major role in regulating aviation security.[1] And, though the attacks of September 11 resulted from a globalized threat—the hijackers were foreign members of a global terrorist network—this chapter takes a national perspective on aviation security. The attacks involved domestic flights, prompting federal policymakers to strengthen aviation security in the United States. Before that day, aviation security measures were comparatively modest and reactive; the terrorist attacks against the Pentagon and the World Trade Center led to drastic measures.

The following analysis provides more ground to the claim that political leaders can manipulate public fears to their advantage. After the attacks of September 11, the Bush Administration actively participated in the construction of collective insecurity, engaging in a dual discourse on terrorism. On one hand, the administration constantly reminded the population of the existence of terrorist threats, most notably through the creation of an alert system. On the other hand, the administration depicted itself as a strong source of protection against terrorism, allowing President Bush to encourage people to return to their normal lives. This dual message was part of a Republican electoral strategy that emphasized both the presence of the terrorist threat and the necessity for strong Republican leadership, depicted as the only genuine source of security in this era of global terrorism.

Terrorism and Aviation Security
before September 11

Terrorist threats to commercial aviation were known long before September 11. The first midair terrorist bombing of a commercial aircraft occurred in 1949, and less than two decades later the first politically motivated terrorist hijacking took place in 1968. That same year, hijackers staged the first armed assault on a commercial plane on the ground. In the late 1960s and the 1970s, the number of attacks on airports and commercial planes rose sharply before reaching a peak during the 1980s. After 1986, the number of terrorist attacks on commercial aviation declined significantly. Between 1947 and 1996, "there were 1,098 attacks on airliners, compared with 129 attacks on airports and 249 attacks on airline offices."[2] Though most of these attacks were hijackings, few resulted in casualties; most of these hijackings were conducted either as a way for hijackers to escape from a threatening situation, or as a means for them to extort money and other resources.

Much rarer than hijackings, in-air bombings were much deadlier as well, accounting for nearly 74 percent of the 2,752 casualties related to attacks against airliners recorded between 1947 and 1996. Yet this figure is extremely small when compared with the growing number of passengers and flights during these decades.[3] In the 1990s, aviation safety reached what some experts labeled a "golden age." In the case of first-world domestic commercial flights, the death risk per flight between 1990 and 1999 averaged only 1 in 13 million. During that period, the chance of dying from an in-air terrorist attack remained minuscule—1 in 2 billion for international flights, and nonexistent for American domestic flights—with the large majority of aviation deaths resulting from accidents, not terrorist acts.[4]

Despite these reassuring statistics, terrorist acts, with the help of the media that feature them prominently, can induce much—legitimate—fear in the public's mind. As noted, airline travel generates insecurity because passengers give up their autonomy during the flight: they must trust in the pilots, the airline companies, and the state regulations that are supposed to guarantee their safety. Moreover, plane crashes may kill hundreds of people simultaneously, and the odds of surviving a plane crash are low. When a major plane crash occurs, demands for new safety measures suddenly increase. In most cases, these demands decline over time as the event fades from public consciousness, until the next spectacular crash.[5] Before the events of September 11, in the United States and abroad, the cyclical nature of airline regulation politics concerned both accidents and terror-ist acts.

The American debate on aviation security before September 11 is ex-emplified by the Lockerbie crash of 1988. On December 21, Pan Am Flight 103, a Boeing 747 carrying 259 passengers, departed from London's Heathrow airport bound for New York and Detroit. Less than forty min-utes into the flight, the plane exploded over Lockerbie, Scotland. All pas-sengers and crewmembers died, in addition to eleven residents of Locker-bie who were struck by falling debris. This spectacular catastrophe initiated major cross-national investigations.[6] Soon after the explosion, it became clear that a bomb had destroyed the plane. More than a decade after the tragedy, two Libyan intelligence agents, Abdelbaset al-Megrahi and Al-Amin Khalifa Fhimah, went on trial; Al-Megrahi was convicted and jailed for life, but Fhimah was acquitted. In May 2002, Libya offered compensa-tion to families of the victims of this tragedy.[7]

In the months following the Lockerbie disaster, friends and relatives of its American victims formed a vocal group that lobbied Congress and the president to conduct a public inquiry into the bombing. On August 4, 1989, President George H. W. Bush responded to their demands by estab-lishing the President's Commission on Aviation Security and Terrorism (PCAST), whose goal was to evaluate current practices and policy alterna-tives dealing with the prevention of aviation terrorism with a focus on the destruction of Pan Am Flight 103.[8] Their final report criticized both Pan Am and the Federal Aviation Administration (FAA) for inappropriate re-sponses to aviation terrorist threats. According to the commission, the Lockerbie catastrophe could have been prevented with a more compre-hensive aviation security system. The report recommended revamping the American aviation security system, calling for a far-reaching assessment of security threats at domestic airports.[9] The commission also called for the establishment of an Assistant Secretary of Transportation, a new position in the federal administration that would deal with intelligence and avia-tion security. This recommendation was rapidly acted on, as were several others in the report.[10]

Despite the push for reform that followed the Lockerbie disaster, Con-gress did not enact comprehensive airline security legislation in the early 1990s. Furthermore, the FAA failed to apply several provisions of the Avi-ation Security Act of 1990, the main aviation security legislation adopted at the time. Elected officials and airline companies adopted a purely reac-tive approach to security, enacting piecemeal reforms only in response to specific incidents.[11]

Several factors explain this reactive approach. First, in a fragmented in-stitutional context that empowers interest groups, the airline industry is an influential and well-organized lobby on Capitol Hill. Though airline companies need to reassure the public about flight safety and security, the issue of cost control is crucial to them. Many security measures are expensive and, before the events of September 11, airline companies covered most of the costs. These companies thus had a vested interest in delaying or watering down proposed improvements to aviation security, especially the most expensive ones.[12]

Second, the FAA took only minimal action against airlines that failed to respect new federal norms and recommendations, instead of confronting them or dealing out harsh penalties. This attitude may have been related to the contradictory mandate of the FAA, regulating and promoting airline traffic simultaneously.[13] This ambiguous institutional status is similar to that of the British MAFF (discussed in the previous chapter).

Third, before September 11, "consumers did not have security on the top of their list of aviation concerns, only wanting to get to their destination as quickly as possible."[14] Facing little public pressure to act, Congress had no incentive to take bold actions during the 1990s to fight aviation terrorism, especially since in that decade the number of terrorist attacks against airplanes declined.[15]

In July 1996, TWA Flight 800, a Boeing 747 carrying 230 passengers, exploded mysteriously over Long Island Sound, and the issue of aviation security was once again on policymakers' agendas. Despite a lack of evidence, journalists and members of the public began speculating on a link between terrorism and the explosion, theorizing that a bomb or missile may have destroyed the plane. To show a commitment to aviation security, President Bill Clinton launched the White House Commission on Aviation Safety and Security. Most of the fifty-seven recommendations from its final report, issued on February 12, 1997,[16] were never implemented.

> The primary contribution of the commission was not to make air traffic safer but to create the perception that action was forthcoming. A year later, when a status report was issued, terrorism was not a primary concern, and attention to commission recommendations waned.[17]

Aviation security gradually fell off the notoriously unstable policy agenda. The low probability of terrorist attacks and the mobilization of the airline industry against costly security measures led policymakers to enact only limited measures, such as baggage screening, background checks on security personnel, matching bags with passengers, and asking passengers whether they had packed their luggage themselves. Aviation security did not reemerge as a vital policy issue until September 11, 2001, and only the catastrophic events of that day, and the lingering sense of national crisis that followed, would durably maintain the issue's position on the federal policy agenda.

After September 11: Global Terrorism and the New Politics of Aviation Security

The terrorist attacks of September 11 manifested the dark side of globalization, and their widespread economic and political consequences reshaped the politics of aviation security in the United States. The attacks crushed the airline industry; during the first week after the tragedy alone, the industry lost more than two billion dollars, and three months later many potential passengers were still afraid to board airplanes, which were flying half-empty.[18] Following the attacks, many United States-based airlines announced enormous layoffs—US Airlines and United Airlines laid off about 20,000 employees each—and Boeing, the Seattle-based airplane maker, announced that it would lay off more than 30,000 of its workers. The terrorist attacks also damaged business for foreign airlines, because "airlines feed passengers to each other, and are interconnected."[19] Furthermore, the hotel and tourism industry directly suffered from this decline in the number of airline travelers, as did the American economy as a whole. These events precipitated massive losses in American stock markets, and sales of most products and services declined.

Sales did increase, however, for some items: guns, gasmasks, American flags, bottled water, cellular phones, life insurance policies, and surveillance equipment were all sold in enormous quantities.[20] The increased sales of these items indicate the high level of collective insecurity prevailing at the time. The media participated in the construction of this acute sense of insecurity through incessant alarming reports on new terrorist threats.

Politicians helped to construct this insecurity as well. The Bush Administration issued many terror alerts in the months and years following the attacks, and on March 12, 2002, unveiled a color-coded scale to aid in dispensing this information. Reminding the population about the terrorist threat on a regular basis may have kept citizens vigilant in watching for potential threats, but it simultaneously boosted the President's popularity as well.[21] The administration successfully framed the threat in a way that kept citizens on alert while constantly reminding them about the good work being done in the White House to protect them.

The attacks of September 11 also shifted the attention of policymakers and the airline industry from the issue of aviation *safety* to aviation *security*. Before the attacks, safety was the more prominent policy issue, but after September 11 security became an obsession.[22] In addition to the growing fear of terrorism, three factors explain this shift.

First, the airline industry was losing billions of dollars and wanted urgently to restore the public's trust in airport and aviation security. Second, the issue of aviation security now seemed closely tied to national security as the world discovered that large airplanes could become terrifying and deadly "weapons of mass destruction."[23] From this perspective, the threat infrastructure and the related meaning of aviation security evolved: in addition to protecting passengers and crew members, aviation security now prevented terrorists from transforming commercial airplanes into missiles capable of destroying civilian and military targets. Played over and over again on television and over the Internet, images of the planes crashing into the Twin Towers of the Wolrd Trade Center amplified this fear of airplanes falling bomb-like from the sky, killing the innocent people inside and on the ground.

Third, the four flights hijacked on September 11 were domestic, not international. Thus, no one could blame the success of the attacks on security loopholes at foreign airports. This increased pressure on federal policymakers as well as American airports and airliners to address the issue of terrorism directly. If reinforced international cooperation to fight terrorism became a crucial issue after September 11, the first priority for federal policymakers was enacting comprehensive measures against airline terrorism at home. Without the swift enactment of such measures, public confidence in aviation security would remain low and the industry would suffer even greater loss. Furthermore, the Republican administration faced blame for not having done enough to prevent the attacks.[24] Though the president could (and did) shift some blame to his predecessor, Bush launched an aggressive "War on Terror" that included significant aviation security measures. This was probably the best way to hide the indecisions of the past and to gain electoral credit for restoring some sense of security. Protecting passengers and the general public against airline terrorism appeared as a major step in this new War on Terror that implicitly promoted national and transportation security over personal freedom and hassle-free traveling.[25]

The federal government's first response to the attacks was to close all American airports for several days. Because Washington DC's Reagan National Airport is located so near the Capitol, the Pentagon, and the White House, it remained closed for weeks before reopening with tighter security requirements for arriving and departing flights. The Bush Administration sent thousands of National Guard troops to patrol reopened commercial airports in the days after September 11. There is little evidence that this measure significantly increased aviation security, but for the president, the decision to send troops to commercial airports was a political gesture aimed at reassuring the public about the security of American airports.

In early November 2001, the President declared that the number of National Guard troops patrolling airports would increase from 6,000 to more than 9,000 for the busy Thanksgiving and Christmas holidays. The federal state covered the $270 million cost of what was partly a public relations operation. In early 2002, the Bush Administration announced that uniformed police officers would gradually replace National Guard troops patrolling airports. The federal state planned to "reimburse the airports for the officers' salaries."[26]

Immediately after the attacks, the FAA took other measures to tighten existing security in the airports, from restricting parking around airports to having passengers show picture identification before boarding. Furthermore, passengers could not carry knives, box cutters, ice picks, or other potential weapons inside the planes. On September 22, only eleven days after the attacks, Congress also granted the American airline industry $15 billion in the form of low-interest loans ($10 billion) and cash grants ($5 billion).[27] This money came on top of a $3 billion subsidy to improve aviation security that was part of the $40 billion emergency legislation enacted the week before. According to the president, the new legislation supporting the airline industry would "provide urgently needed tools to assure the safety and immediate stability of our nation's commercial airline system." This corporate welfare was a key element of the War on Terror: "The terrorists who attacked our country on September 11 will not shut down our vital businesses or thwart our way of life."[28] By then, this defiant nationalist tone had become a trademark of the Republican administration, shaping the perception of the threat against which they claimed to protect the population.

The strong sense of national crisis and collective insecurity prevailing after September 11 created an atmosphere of legislative emergency that led to the enactment of several major relief and security bills. The idea that the country was under attack favored the creation of a bipartisan mood in Congress, but this did not mean that a consensus had emerged over policy preferences, including those related to the so-called War on Terror. In the context of divided government, the absence of party discipline and fragmentation of power at the federal level meant that compromise still seemed necessary to enact new legislation. Moreover, the two parties in Congress wanted to receive credit for measures aimed at protecting the population and the airline industry. September 11 did not abolish electoral competition; it only altered its meaning.

As for the political behavior of the airline industry, it moved to address changing circumstances. Considering their financial loss, the industry understood the need for bold actions to reinforce security in its sector. Because of their adverse financial situation, however, airlines could hardly assume the full burden of the proposed security measures. From their perspective, the federal state had to step in to help the industry and to make travelers feel safe. These issues are essential to understanding the legislative history of the most significant aviation antiterrorism bill adopted in Congress after September 11: the Airport Security Federalization Act.

The Senate moved first to draft a comprehensive bill on aviation security. Going beyond the measures adopted immediately after September 11, the Senate proposed to increase drastically the number of armed sky marshals traveling on domestic flights. More important, most senators—especially Democrats—supported the federalization of the more than 28,000 baggage-screening jobs at airport security checkpoints across the country. In this plan, these new federal employees would work under the supervision of the Department of Justice, which would be in charge of airport security in the United States. The main reason the federalization of airport screeners moved onto the federal policy agenda was that private security companies, though not held responsible for the September 11 attacks, still faced strong criticism for lack of proper training and background checks for their employees.[29] These highly publicized issues helped Democrats in Congress promote the federalization of the airport security business. Federalization clearly served the traditional Democratic agenda, which generally favors the expansion of the federal state in American society.

Emphasizing the swiftness of their antiterrorism efforts, Senate members raced to complete work on the bill by October 11, exactly one month after the attacks.[30] Despite deep reservations about the federalization of baggage screeners, conservative Republicans finally supported the proposed measures, in part because a Gallup survey showed that a large majority of the population supported a complete federal takeover of baggage screening. Democrats used this survey to convince Republicans to support federalization and the bill on airport security. The Senate finally passed the bill 100 to 0.[31]

Meanwhile, members of the House of Representatives had been studying the issue of aviation security. Supported by the White House, a Republican bill that did not include the federalization of baggage screeners was put forward. This bill was adopted 286 to 139. Sixty-nine of those who supported the bill were Democrats, showing that to avoid future blame for their apparent inaction, many Democrats "were prepared to vote for almost any type of aviation security bill."[32]

In the conference committee, debate over the federalization of airport screeners raged. Republican senators expressed second thoughts about this provision, but by that time it was difficult to reject a bill enacted without opposition in the Senate. Since the majority of the population seemed to support the federalization of screeners, if no measure was adopted and if there were new attacks, citizens and journalists could blame elected officials—especially Republicans.

> What if there was another airline terrorist attack while they were bickering over public vs. private baggage screeners? That would be nothing short of a political disaster. So even though some GOP lawmakers strongly believed that private screeners would make the system safer than government screeners, they went along with the Senate.[33]

To avoid potential blame for inaction, many elected officials supported a measure they did not truly believe was the best way to protect the public.

Ironically, though Republicans generally oppose direct federal intervention in the private sector, they participated in this expansion of "big government," as more than 28,000 new civil servants joined the federal workforce. In the name of national security, President Bush signed this legislation on November 19, 2001, contradicting traditional conservative beliefs against "big government." In his speech on that day, the president invoked the strong emphasis on security that had quickly become dominant in American aviation policy, stressing bipartisanship and political unity in the face of the terrorist threat:

> The broad support for this bill shows that our country is united in this crisis. We have our political differences, but we're united to defend our country. And we're united to protect our people. For our airways, there is one supreme priority: Security.[34]

The President also enumerated the most significant provisions of the legislation, reassuring the public on aviation security in the post–September 11 world:

> For the first time, airport security will become a direct federal responsibility. Overseen by a new Under Secretary of Transportation for Security. Additional funds will be provided for federal air marshals. And a new team of federal security managers, supervisors, law enforcement officers and screeners will ensure all passengers and carry-on bags are inspected thoroughly and effectively. The new security force will be well-trained, made up of US citizens. And if any of its members do not perform, the new Under Secretary will have full authority to discipline or remove them.[35]

Though doubts remain on the effectiveness of the Airport Security Federalization Act in fighting terrorism, this legislation does expand the role of the federal state in the field of aviation security and transportation regulation. The legislation significantly increases the size the federal workforce while sending a message to the public that the federal state is largely responsible for aviation security. Paradoxically, if new airline terrorist attacks were to occur, federal officials would now find it more difficult to escape blame, because after September 11 they reassured the public about aviation security with these measures. This is perhaps why members of Congress from both parties have already distanced themselves from the newly created Transportation Security Administration, the regulatory agency in charge of aviation security. This way, if new attacks do occur, members of Congress can deflect blame onto an agency that Republican Representative John Mica of Florida linked to "Soviet-style centralized bureaucracy."[36]

Despite this distancing from politicians, the Transportation Security Administration and other post–September 11 aviation security measures have received massive popular support because most citizens are willing to pay the price for what is described as improved aviation security. Because flying in the post–September 11 world worries many passengers, they are willing to wait longer in line and to sacrifice some of their personal freedom and travel time.

What is true for post–September 11 aviation security, however, is not necessarily so for other forms of state protection. As evidenced in Chapter One, citizens sometimes feel that the state imposes excessive constraints and that the related reduction in personal freedom is unacceptable. In the case of gun control in the United States, the National Rifle Association and other organizations depict most proposed gun legislations as illegitimate attacks on personal freedom and Constitutional rights. And in the field of transportation regulation, auto safety provides an interesting contrast with the post–September 11 politics of aviation security. For many drivers, existing speed limits and the obligation to wear safety belts represent unacceptable infringements on personal freedom. Libertarians even attack the very idea of state intervention in the field of auto safety:

> People should be allowed to use only seat belts if they want. Car manufacturers shouldn't be forced to install air bags. Politicians could even admit they didn't know what they were doing, and take themselves completely out of the automotive safety business.[37]

This type of argument has some currency because, for many people, the car remains a powerful symbol of personal freedom that the state should not have control over. Here, the difference with aviation security is striking, as passengers who enter a plane implicitly agree to give away most of their personal freedom temporarily and to depend on pilots and other crew members for their safety. As opposed to the car, the plane is a symbol of our dependency on other human beings and of our willingness to sacrifice our personal freedom temporarily in the name of collective safety. The events of September 11 have reinforced this perception, which explains why passengers agree to enter the long and sometimes humiliating screening process. Those unwilling to do that can decide not to fly. Still, the example of post–September 11 aviation security should not hide that state protection is sometimes imposed on citizens who are skeptical about the need for specific forms of state protection.

Discussion

It is difficult to assess the impact of the Airport Security Federalization Act on aviation security.[38] Federal screeners have been in place since November 2002. Although better paid than they were when they worked for private security companies, these screeners are not much better trained than before. The Airport Security Federalization Act, an attempt to make the public feel safer about air travel, may not have done nearly as much as politicians had promised to improve aviation security; even after the implementation of the legislation, airport screening has regularly failed to detect dangerous items hidden in carry-on bags.[39] Although baggage screening is certainly more effective than before the September 11 attacks, significant security challenges remain, fueling ongoing debates about aviation security.[40]

Furthermore, the post–September 11 shift from safety to security could have a negative effect in the long run. As Roger Cobb and David Primo note, "plane crashes can divert resources away from safety issues that have not yet resulted in an accident. Similarly, aviation security can divert resources away from crash prevention."[41] Aviation safety and security legislation in the United States and abroad is thus reactive, mainly because of tactics of blame avoidance: when a crash occurs, policymakers and airline companies attempt to reassure the public about aviation safety while avoiding blame for future accidents that might have the same perceived cause.

There is no evidence that the events of September 11 altered this logic, but these attacks kept issues of aviation safety and security on the policy agenda for much longer than had previous incidents such as the crashes of Pan Am Flight 103 and TWA Flight 800. The enormity of the September 11 attacks and their hugely negative impact on the airline industry created a sense of national crisis that permitted the federal state to take over most of the business of aviation protection. Without this aggravated sense of national crisis, institutional obstacles to reform, like checks and balances, would likely have prevented this transformation from occurring. The greater involvement of the federal state in the business of aviation security could paradoxically increase the electoral risks that future air-based terrorist attacks could bring about. If such attacks take place, the more central role of the federal state in aviation security could amplify the blame that federal civil servants and elected officials face.

After September 11, the Bush Administration framed a dual discourse about terrorism. On one hand, President Bush attempted to comfort the public and to proclaim that every effort was being made to prevent another attack; on the other, the president exploited the prevailing sense of collective insecurity in order to promote his administration's agenda and to boost his popular support at home. Stressing the apparent effectiveness of the new security measures he supported, the president constantly reminded citizens about the terrorist threat. The Bush Administration parlayed their popular success with domestic security policy into foreign affairs, linking terrorism to their push for war in Iraq. The alert system put together by the new Department of Homeland Security reinforced this sense of menace, which is superimposed on a discourse on the need to return to normal life in the reassuring context of increased security measures. These remarks exemplify once again the central role of political leaders in the construction of collective insecurity and state protection. As Tilly's state building theory suggests, these actors participate in the construction of the threats against which they claim to protect the public. In the case of the United States, the Bush Administration focused mainly on a narrow vision of state protection centered on national security at the expense of major environmental and social problems, leaving many of these issues to the private sector and nonprofit organizations.[42]

Unfortunately for the president and the Republican Party, ten months after the 2004 presidential election, public and media outcry over their slow response to the Hurricane Katrina disaster in New Orleans seriously tarnished their carefully built image as relentless national defenders. Although local and state officials shared the blame for that slow response, President Bush's apparent indecision in the aftermath of this catastrophe eroded the credibility of an administration that already faced mounting criticism about American losses in Iraq.[43]

This chapter's analysis of the politics of aviation security illustrates the five claims formulated in Chapter Four. First, the analysis stresses once again the limitations of the concept of moral panic, whose application to the post–September 11 debate over aviation security is problematic. The attacks may have created a sense of national crisis that Republicans exploited for political gain, but both the crisis and the insecurity that citizens felt afterwards had their basis in reality. Indeed, the threat of another serious terrorist attack proved real, with major incidents outside the United States, including the Madrid bombings of March 2004 and the London bombings of July 2005. The genuine, profound nature of the terrorist threat is not consistent with a strict moral panic argument, in which the threat is necessarily inflated.

Second, this chapter offers another clear example of the increasing risk awareness of the population—i.e., most Americans now know that terrorism is a major potential threat—as well as the lasting reliance of citizens and interest groups on state protection—in this case, their push to federalize airport security.

Third, this case shows how political leaders use the perception of collective threats to increase their electoral support. In the case of aviation security, the threat infrastructure of this policy area, i.e., the spectacular nature of plane crashes, makes these strategies especially profitable for ruling political leaders, who can depict themselves as the best defenders of ordinary citizens against global "evildoers." Aviation terrorism, moreover, is a great source of political risk, which explains why elected officials must respond to it in an apparently bold manner.

Fourth, as evidenced by the massive political concerns about the sustainability of the American aviation industry, powerful economic interests can become major players in the politics of insecurity. Finally, this case again exemplifies the distinction between reactive and proactive strategies. Before the 2001 attacks, elected officials adopted a purely reactive approach both in terms of discourse and policy approach. After the attacks, policymaking remained reactive, but the Bush Administration adopted increasingly proactive behavior, attempting to shape the perception of the terrorist threat and to keep it on the agenda in order to generate positive electoral results for the Republican Party. As the 2002 and 2004 electoral results suggest, such political construction of terrorism-related insecurity proved successful in the short run.[44] This winning political strategy was tied to the idea of globalization, as many elected officials depicted the United States as the victim of a global terrorist conspiracy that only bold state power, international cooperation, and military interventions abroad could eradicate.[45] This case illustrates the relationship between globalization, collective insecurity, and state protection, discussed further in Chapter Three.

Notes

1. The International Civil Aviation Organization (ICAO) was founded in 1944 and operates under the United Nations. On the history and role of this organization in the postwar era, see Eugene Sochor (1991), *The Politics of International Aviation* (London: Macmillan).

2. Most of these attacks did not lead to human casualties. See Ariel Merari (1999), "Attacks on Civil Aviation: Trends and Lessons," in Paul Wilkinson and Brian M. Jenkins, eds., *Aviation Terrorism and Security* (London: Frank Cass), pp. 9–29.
3. Ibid., p. 18.
4. A. Barnett (2001), "Air Safety: End of the Golden Age?" *Journal of the Operational Research Society* 52: 849–54 (851).
5. See Roger W. Cobb and David M. Primo (2003), *The Plane Truth: Airline Crashes, the Media, and Transportation Policy* (Washington, DC: Brookings Institution), and Thomas A. Birkland (2004), "Learning and Policy Improvement after Disaster: The Case of Aviation Security," *American Behavioral Scientist* 48(3): 341–64.
6. Peter St. John (1999), "The Politics of Aviation Terrorism," in Paul Wilkinson and Brian M. Jenkins, eds., *Aviation Terrorism and Security* (London: Frank Cass), pp. 27–53 (36).
7. At the time, the Libyan government of Colonel Gaddafi still denied any direct responsibility in the bombing. See BBC News (2002), "Libya 'not to blame' for Lockerbie," June 24 (available online at news.bbc.co.uk/2/hi/middle_east/2062236.stm [accessed March 2007]).
8. For the executive order that created this Commission, see www.presidency.ucsb.edu/ws/print.php?pid=23534 (accessed March 2007).
   See also Rodney Wallis (1993), *Combating Air Terrorism* (Washington, DC: Brassey's), p. 33.
9. See Don Phillips and George Lardner Jr. (1990), "Laxity by Pan Am, FAA Blamed in Jet Bombing," *Washington Post*, May 16, A01, and the President's Commission on Aviation Security and Terrorism (1990), Report to the President (Washington, DC: PCAST).
10. Wallis, *Combating Air Terrorism*, p. 34.
11. Cobb and Primo, *The Plane Truth*, pp. 125–26.
   For a more "optimistic" interpretation of the learning process that follows plane crashes, see Birkland, "Learning and Policy Improvement after Disaster."
12. Cobb and Primo, *The Plane Truth*, pp. 125–26.
13. Ibid., p. 123. The promotion mandate of the FAA no longer exists.
14. Ibid., p. 127.
15. Barnett, "Air Safety," p. 851.
16. White House Commission on Aviation Safety and Security (1997), Report to the President (Washington, DC: The Commission).
17. Cobb and Primo, *The Plane Truth*, p. 111.
18. J. N. Goodrich (2002), "September 11, 2001 Attack on America: A Record of the Immediate Impacts and Reactions in the USA Travel and Tourism Industry," *Tourism Management* 23: 573–80.
19. Ibid.

20. Ibid., p. 577.

21. Robb Willer (2004), "The Effects of Government-Issued Terror Warnings on Presidential Approval Ratings," *Current Research in Social Psychology* 10(1), September (available online at www.uiowa.edu/ %7Egrpproc/crisp/crisp10_1.pdf [accessed March 2007]).

22. This was true for other advanced industrial countries as well; in Canada, for example, significant airline security measures have been enacted since the events of September 11. See Transport Canada (2002), "Transportation Safety and Security" (available online at www.tc.gc.ca/ pol/en/Report/anre2002/4B_e.htm [accessed March 2007]).

23. Cobb and Primo, *The Plane Truth*, p. 131.

24. See, for example, Michael Beschloss (2001), "Bush Faces the Greatest Test," *New York Times*, September 17, p. A15.

25. Perry A. Russell and Frederick W. Preston claim that the "primary un-intended consequence of increased security is surely a reduction in both perceived and real freedoms of the flying public." See Russell and Preston (2004), "Airline Security after the Event," *American Behavioral Scientist* 47(11), July: 1419–27 (1424).

   On the tensions between freedom, efficiency (hassle-free traveling), and security after September 11, see W. Kip Viscusi and Richard J. Zeck-hauser (2003), *Journal of Risk and Uncertainty* 26(2/3): 99–120.

26. *USA Today* (2002), "Policy to Replace Guard at Airports," January 4 (available online at www.usatoday.com/news/sept11/2002/04/01/ airport-security.htm [accessed March 2007]).

27. Cobb and Primo, *The Plane Truth*, p. 132.

28. Cited in BBC News (2001), "Airlines Receive $15bn Aid Boost," September 23 (available online at news.bbc.co.uk/1/hi/business/ 1558854.stm [accessed March 2007]).

29. Even before the attacks, reports had disclosed such problems. See Kathleen M. Sweet (2004), *Aviation and Airport Security* (Upper Saddle River, NJ: Prentice Hall), pp. 177–78.

30. Byron York (2002), "The World That Didn't Change—Much: Partisanship and the Politics of National Security after 9/11," in Wladyslaw Pleszczynski, ed., *Our Brave New World: Essays on the Impact of September 11* (Stanford: Hoover Institution Press): 21–40 (30).

31. Ibid., p. 31.

32. Ibid., p. 32.

33. Ibid., p. 33.

34. President George W. Bush (2001), *Remarks by the President at Signing of Aviation Security Legislation*, November 19 (Washington, DC: Office of the Press Secretary; available online at www.whitehouse.gov/news/ releases/2001/11/20011119-2.html [accessed March 2007]).

35. Ibid.

36. Quoted in David M. Primo and Roger W. Cobb (2004), "Learn from the TSA's Shortcomings," *The Hill*, June 15 (available online at www.hillnews.com/op_ed/061504_tsa.aspx [accessed March 2007]).

37. Libertarian Party (2004), "Libertarian Solutions: Air bags: safety equipment or legislated killers?" (available online at www.lp.org/lpnews/article_402.shtml [accessed March 2007]).

38. On this issue, see Sweet, *Aviation and Airport Security*.

39. The testimony of a former baggage screener who worked for the Transportation Security Administration for three years stresses the problems of some airport screening policies implemented after September 11. See Scott Wallace (2006), " 'Security' without Sense," *Washington Post*, February 19, p. B08.

40. See, for example, Patrick Smith (2006), "Is Airport Security Futile?" on Salon.com (www.salon.com/opinion/feature/2006/08/17/airport_futility/index_np.html [accessed March 2007]).

41. Cobb and Primo, *The Plane Truth*, p. 141.

42. On the formation of the narrow, highly conservative Republican domestic policy agenda, see Jacob S. Hacker and Paul Pierson (2005), *Off Center: The Republican Revolution and the Erosion of American Democracy* (New Haven, CT: Yale University Press).

43. Jonathan Weisman and Michael Abramowitz (2006), "Katrina's Damage Lingers For Bush: Many See Storm as President's Undoing," *Washington Post*, August 26, p. A01.

44. But popular support for the Republican domestic agenda remains limited; ibid.

It would be simplistic to argue that the politics of insecurity is the only factor that explains the outcome of the 2004 presidential election. For an overview of the 2005 presidential campaign see William Crotty, ed., *A Defining Moment: The Presidential Election of 2004* (Armonk, NY: M. E. Sharpe), and Larry J. Sabato, ed. (2005), *Divided States of America: The Slash and Burn Politics of the 2004 Presidential Election* (New York: Longman Publishing).

45. On this issue, see Benjamin R. Barber (2003), *Fear's Empire: War, Terrorism, and Democracy* (New York: W. W. Norton), and Byron Miller (2005), *The Globalization of Fear* (unpublished paper; Calgary: University of Calgary).

Insecurity and Electoral Competition

Crime is still a major concern of citizens in advanced industrial societies, and politicians address this issue on a regular basis. Since the 1980s, the "get-tough," "zero tolerance" approach to crime has gained ideological ground. Though the United States is widely perceived internationally as the most fertile soil for crime and for the implementation of zero tolerance policies, these issues are concerns in other advanced industrial countries as well. Media outlets, think tanks, and international policy networks have spread the idea of zero tolerance across the planet, showing once again the role of globalization in the politics of insecurity.[1]

In the debate over national insecurity during the French 2002 presidential campaign, zero tolerance toward urban delinquency became a major policy issue. In France, "insecurity" refers primarily, but not exclusively, to the negative effects of youth delinquency in deprived suburbs, where many housing projects are located. Acts commonly linked to urban delinquency, such as graffiti, car burnings, and other forms of vandalism, are known in France as "incivilities." The insecurity is tied to globalization and immigration, and the *Front national* (FN), a far right political party, has long blamed immigrants for increases in insecurity and criminal activities.

Insecurity became the main topic of the political debate in the early 2000s for several reasons. First, crime statistics showed a long-term increase in delinquency and other types of criminal activities. Second, police labor unions mobilized to push for zero tolerance policies. Third, media coverage, overly sympathetic to police grievances, sensationalized criminal activities and their consequences. And fourth, French President Jacques Chirac, running for reelection, engaged in a dramatic discourse on crime, blaming left-wing politicians for their incapacity to fight the problem effectively.

The national focus on insecurity damaged the campaign of the main left-wing candidate, Lionel Jospin. The results of the first ballot were an enormous surprise: Jospin was eliminated from the race, and xenophobic candidate Jean-Marie Le Pen finished second. Le Pen faced Chirac in the second round, and following a great social and political mobilization against Le Pen, Chirac easily won the election.

After Chirac's reelection, the French parliament adopted zero tolerance legislation in order to reinforce "law and order." Although France did not embrace the American model of vast incarceration, the 2002 campaign created a need to reform the French judiciary system. The reforms would follow a more conservative vision of law enforcement, focusing on punishment instead of rehabilitation.

This chapter's analysis of Chirac and Le Pen and their behavior during the 2002 election shows how politicians affect the insecurity agenda and the perception of collective threats as part of their electoral strategies. Moreover, Le Pen's pessimistic discourse on immigration stresses the potential role of globalization, and discourse on globalization, in the politics of insecurity.

Unemployment, Immigration, and Insecurity

During the 1980s and 1990s, unemployment and, to a lesser extent, immigration were the most debated policy issues in France. With the unemployment rate frequently above 10 percent, young people found it difficult to enter the labor market, and older workers who lost their jobs could seldom find new ones. High wages and payroll taxes as well as tight labor market regulations made job creation more difficult in France than in Britain and the United States, two countries where labor market flexibility had become the dominant economic creed. Despite efforts to facilitate the hiring of young workers, long-term unemployment affected a significant portion of the population.

Long-term unemployment had a negative effect on French youth, especially those living in housing projects located in the deprived suburbs (*banlieues*) of Paris, Lyon, Marseille, Strasbourg, and other major French cities.[2] Immigrants from Africa and their descendants are disproportionately represented in these suburbs. Although vague, the term "exclusion" came to define the situation of many citizens who could not find a stable job and, for that reason, could not enter mainstream French society. The geographical isolation of these deprived suburbs reinforced the idea that France was witnessing the advent of a divided society that betrayed the egalitarian model of citizenship at the center of the French republican tradition.

> The very word *la banlieue*, which creates an image of crime and indigence, graffiti and burned-down cars cut off from Paris and other French cities highlights the extends to which the extreme deprivation of segments of French society is marginal to the majority's daily existence and life chances.[3]

Social and economic problems like unemployment bred ethnic tensions, as a portion of the population with African backgrounds felt increasingly left behind. This situation triggered a debate over the efficiency of the "French model of integration" based on secularism and color-blind public policy.[4] A large portion of the immigrant population came from North Africa and belonged to Islam, which exacerbated ethnic tensions in a predominantly Catholic society where the law draws a clear distinction between the state and organized religion.[5] The widely-publicized debate over the wearing of Islamic head scarves in France's officially secular public schools added to concerns about the future of the "French model of integration" and, more specifically, about the status of immigrants and citizens of North African descent in contemporary France.[6]

Despite this focus on unemployment and immigration, crime was a significant policy issue during the 1980s and the 1990s. Traditionally, right-wing parties identified themselves with law enforcement issues, accusing left-wing politicians of adopting a permissive approach to crime and delinquency. In 1981, the left came to power for the first time since the 1958 establishment of the Fifth Republic. Despite efforts to prevent delinquency through community-based programs, periodical explosions of violence in some deprived suburbs provided right-wing politicians with opportunities to blame the left for the decline of social order and the rise of what the French came to label as insecurity. In the narrow sense of the term, the French refer to insecurity as the fear of crime and delinquency, rather than its broader meaning of a general sense of anxiety and uncertainty.

The vague meaning of the widely debated idea of insecurity created a window of opportunity for right-wing politicians. Although the following remark applies specifically to the strategy of Jacques Chirac during the 2002 presidential campaign, it shows how a vague idea can bring people together against a common threat that is never clearly defined:

> The issue of insecurity was for all intents and purposes a storyline that could be manipulated . . . to mean different things for different constituencies. It

offered the possibility of bringing together a coalition of those concerned with rising crime, and those being left behind by urban decline, or feeling threatened by globalization and fears of change.[7]

However, because unemployment remained the most crucial policy issue of the 1980s and 1990s, insecurity, in the narrow sense of the term, was not a factor in most political debates and electoral campaigns. The extent to which mainstream right-wing politicians could exploit the issue during these decades remained limited.

On the far right, however, populist politician Jean-Marie Le Pen extensively used growing concerns about crime, unemployment, and globalization in order to gain more electoral ground. His openly xenophobic party, the *Front national* (FN), put forward the idea that immigration represented the root cause of all social and economic problems, including delinquency and insecurity.

> At the national level, the words "immigration" and "insecurity" are almost hyphenated in FN discourse—so close is the perceived relationship between the two issues. The same is true at the provincial level, where the issue of law and order is automatically linked to the question of immigration.[8]

Supporting the false claim that immigrants are behind most criminal acts, FN officials referred to crime data in a selective and misleading manner. FN publications depicted French cities and subways as dangerous zones where "organized ethnic bands" terrorized innocent citizens.[9] Exploiting collective anxieties related to globalization and immigration, the FN blamed immigrants and their descendants for what it described as an unparalleled crime wave. Paradoxically, this framing of the issue of insecurity reduced the anxieties of many FN supporters:

> In the case of feelings of growing personal insecurity, the ideology may provide a means of reducing the diffuse fear and anxiety arising from not knowing what or whom to fear. Since a belief that immigrants are criminal, for instance, may reduce the level of experienced uncertainty (i.e., "you know whom you should look out for"), it may have seemingly positive effects on individuals living under this kind of stress.[10]

Public opinion surveys in the 1990s showed that FN supporters, who were overrepresented in the working class, felt more insecure about the future than did supporters of other parties, and FN supporters were on average more concerned about crime and security than the rest of the population.[11] Yet the FN also became popular in rural areas, where far fewer immigrants and youth delinquents live. This suggests that collective insecurity can become an ideological and political construction that is not strongly related to the concrete, everyday experience of citizens. Such logic reflects the threat infrastructure of urban delinquency, a morally charged and potentially spectacular issue that can attract much media attention and, with the help of politicians like Le Pen, make episodes of acute collective insecurity likely.

Le Pen and his party succeeded in portraying themselves as an alternative to mainstream politicians through a populist discourse that targeted voters disillusioned with traditional parties. Perceived as a protest vote against these politicians, who seemed unable to fight unemployment and to restore confidence in the future of the nation, the FN received almost 15 percent of the popular vote at the 1988 and the 1995 first-round presidential elections.[12] These figures and, more generally, the lasting presence of the FN on the French political scene shocked many centrist and left-wing politicians, media commentators, and social activists. In 1984, a social movement fighting racism (*SOS racisme*) emerged, denouncing the FN and its rhetoric. In the following years, moderate political parties refused to forge any formal electoral alliance with the FN. Attempts to marginalize the FN did not succeed, however, as that party maintained a central position in the French political landscape for over fifteen years.

The FN succeeded partially because of grassroots efforts by FN politicians who made their presence felt at the local level, campaigning door-to-door while mobilizing populist rhetoric against what they described as a Paris-based, arrogant political elite. The lasting presence of the FN in the French political landscape embarrassed mainstream right-wing politicians, who condemned Le Pen's xenophobic ideology, and toned down their own rhetoric about "law and order" to avoid sounding like the FN discourse. The FN's presence in the French political arena may have prevented moderate right-wing parties from exploiting this trademark issue of insecurity in order to gain more electoral support. However, this situation changed at the turn of the century, and the issue of insecurity moved to the center of the policy agenda at the same time media commentators perceived a decline in support for the FN.

Before the Campaign: The Agenda Setting Process

Insecurity emerged as a central policy issue in the years and months preceding the 2002 French presidential campaign for several reasons. First, victimization surveys as well as official crime statistics from French police showed that the number of reported "incivilities" and other criminal activities had increased over the previous decade. Pointing to the problematic

nature of these statistics, some scholars argued that the increase in the number of "incivilities" reflected in part a greater level of law-enforcement activity, not a sudden multiplication of delinquent acts.[13] But rising crime figures helped many journalists, politicians, and policy experts validate the emerging common wisdom that insecurity had become a major threat to social order and a legitimate source of concern for citizens and policy-makers alike.[14] Ironically, the decline of unemployment in the late 1990s contributed to a shift in the public's attention from job creation to law enforcement problems.[15]

> As long as the concern about unemployment remained dominant, only a small minority—about 15% of the population—responded that insecurity was the most crucial problem to solve. Yet . . . more than a third of the population was seriously concerned about delinquency, and another third was moderately concerned. With the recent decline of the fears related to unemployment, those who feel very insecure [about delinquency] are less reluctant to express their concerns.[16]

Opinion surveys conducted in the late 1990s and early 2000s confirmed the scope of distress about crime and delinquency. With the decline of unemployment, a growing number of citizens and political leaders depicted insecurity as their number-one priority.[17] As in other countries, these popular concerns about crime stimulated the rapid development of the private security business.[18]

These statistics and increasing popular concern, as well as alarming media reports on the "lawless" situation prevailing in some French suburbs, provided new ideological ammunition to right-wing intellectuals and politicians who had long decried the rise of delinquency and so-called urban violence. Normally, Le Pen's *Front national* would have been the first to gain from this situation, but in the late 1990s, two factors prevented the FN from benefiting from these growing concerns. First, the decline of unemployment temporarily weakened the popularity of a party that had found significant support among the working class. Second, growing divisions over Le Pen's leadership led to a dramatic split in December 1998, with the FN losing Bruno Mégret, a key strategist, and with many supporters leaving to create their own party, the *Front National—Mouvement National*.

With the extreme right thus divided, and polls showing worry about delinquency, President Chirac turned the issue of insecurity against left-wing Prime Minister Jospin, who planned to run against him during the 2002 presidential campaign. As early as 1997, Jospin and his Socialist Party attempted to deflect right-wing blame about their apparently soft stance on crime. During a conference he organized in Villepinte, Jospin framed insecurity—in the narrow sense of the term—as his second most crucial priority after unemployment. To convince his traditional base that the fight against insecurity did not belong only to the right, he referred to a founding document of modern French political culture:

> As stated in the [1789] Declaration of the Rights of Man and Citizen, "security" is one of the "natural and inalienable rights of man." A citizen whose security is not guaranteed cannot exercise his right to freedom. The republican principle of equality between citizens cannot ignore this right to security.[19]

For the Socialist Party, framing the issue of security as a core French principle represented an attempt to deflect potential blame emanating from its own ranks while reinforcing its credibility regarding an issue that right-wing politicians had long used against the left. Jospin's new focus on insecurity thus shielded his coalition government against traditional right-wing attacks regarding the permissive attitude of the left in law enforcement matters. Despite the enactment of legislation on "everyday life security" (*sécurité quotidienne*) in November 2001, the Socialist government of Lionel Jospin did not really implement tough anti-delinquency measures during his mandate (1997–2002). Even with his support for community policing and justice administration, Jospin could hardly embrace comprehensive zero tolerance measures, as this could have destabilized his governmental coalition and his support within the Socialist Party.[20]

The perceived moderation of the Jospin government on the issue of insecurity provided President Chirac with an opportunity to blame the left-wing government with which he had to share power between 1997 and 2002. Despite Jospin's attempt to address the issue, the struggle against crime and insecurity remained a winning topic for the right. In the context of growing popular concerns about insecurity, Chirac made numerous references to this issue in his public speeches. For example, in his traditional New Year's speech of December 31, 1998, he emphasized the respect of law and order as a crucial Republican value, echoing Jospin's above-quoted remark:

> From public officials, my Dear Fellow Citizens, you expect that they enforce law. . . . Security of goods and people is not guaranteed everywhere [in our society]. Education and prevention are crucial yet punishment is as important [as they are]. I remind you that security is the first of all freedoms.[21]

In this speech and others, the President pursued two main objectives: maintaining insecurity on the agenda while reaffirming the right's traditional control over this issue.

In the three years following, the President frequently referred to insecurity, implicitly accusing the Jospin government of inaction in the context of escalating law enforcement concerns. During a television interview on July 14, 2001, Chirac referred to recent crime statistics to dramatize the situation prevailing in France's deprived suburbs, putting Jospin and his other left-wing opponents on the defensive. During this interview, the

President even mentioned that "the rate of violence in France is superior to the one prevailing in the United States."[22] In a country where the United States is widely perceived as overly violent, this remark was a clear attempt to induce anxiety among viewers. This interview as well as presidential speeches on insecurity helped push the issue to the center of French media and political debate.

In the months following this controversial interview, two events helped keep the issue of insecurity on the French policy agenda. First, the terrorist attacks of September 11 in the United States bred popular anxiety in France, which had endured many terrorist bombings during the 1980s and 1990s. Through intense media coverage, the war in Afghanistan and the conflict between Israel and Palestine also affected the popular mood during fall 2001.[23] Demonstrating the link between globalization and the politics of insecurity, events that occurred far away, through media accounts and references to them in political discourse, exacerbated collective insecurity.

Second, police labor unions organized spectacular street protests in October and November of that year. Beyond traditional salary grievances, these protests denounced the weakness of law-enforcement resources after several police officers were injured or killed in street attacks that occurred in poor suburbs.[24] Such protests emphasized a deep malaise within police ranks. Furthermore, the wave of police protests in fall 2001 may have increased media attention towards crime, as the media ran stories about the lack of resources and the "suffering of police officers" (*souffrance policière*). Journalists, especially those working for more conservative outlets like *Le Figaro* and *TF1*, sided with police officers, whose point of view became increasingly dominant in the media discourse on delinquency and "urban violence."[25] In this case, media outlets became *partisan* actors in the politics of insecurity.

This intense media coverage and the mobilization of police unions bolstered right-wing politicians who had long identified with law enforcement issues. The first round of the 2002 presidential campaign focused almost exclusively on law enforcement and insecurity as a result.

The 2002 Presidential Election and Its Aftermath

In France's Fifth Republic, presidents are elected through a second ballot system; only the two candidates who receive the most votes in the first ballot are allowed to run in the second and final round of the campaign.

This electoral system tends to favor a one-on-one race between the left and the right during the last round.[26] In winter 2001, sixteen candidates gathered the 500 signatures necessary to run officially for the presidency. Most of these candidates represented small parties and had no chance to make it to the second round. From the beginning of the campaign, most commentators predicted that Chirac and Jospin would likely face each other in the second round.[27]

But support weakened for Jospin. The great number of left-wing presidential candidates running in the first round divided the vote of the traditional left-wing electorate. Jospin was not a very charismatic candidate, and he alienated his base by stating that the program he represented "was not Socialist."[28] Many traditional left-wing voters were dissatisfied with Jospin and his centrist agenda, and this translated into millions of "protest votes" against him. Many of these voters assumed Jospin would make it to the second round anyway, and during that round most left-wing voters would have probably rallied to support him.[29] Further weakening Jospin's run, insecurity became the central topic of the presidential campaign; this situation clearly favored his right-wing opponents, who had long framed law enforcement as a right-wing issue.

In addition to the longer-term trends mentioned above, the specific context of the mood of late winter and early spring 2002 explained why crime and delinquency became so central during the first round of the French presidential campaign. Media coverage on this insecurity intensified in March and early April 2002, only weeks before the first-round ballot. On television, the number of crime-related stories run in the evening news increased dramatically. Reports dramatized criminal activities while relying mainly on police sources to comment on the situation in France's deprived suburbs.[30] Television journalists often sided with police officers, legitimizing the concerns that police unions had voiced in the fall of 2001. Without much critical distance or reflection, many journalists also reported public outrage about delinquency and fresh police statistics that showed new increases in crime rates. Many media outlets, especially those sympathetic to the right, dramatized the crime situation prevailing in poor suburbs. This populist and catastrophist media coverage seemed to confirm what police officers and right-wing politicians had claimed for years, that social order was on the verge of collapsing and that bold actions were needed to make French society secure again.[31]

In part because it turned the public's attention away from longstanding corruption accusations formulated against him, Chirac welcomed this sensationalist media coverage. For years, he had framed insecurity as a dramatic problem that called for strong right-wing leadership. During his campaign, Chirac focused on insecurity and law enforcement, and media coverage reinforced the apparent legitimacy of his alarmist discourse on the decline of social order in deprived suburbs. Promoting zero tolerance policies against delinquency, he advocated

> the creation of a ministry for Internal Security, regional anti-crime partnerships, a *justice de proximité* (community justice), closed educational centers for young offenders, and new laws to strengthen the powers of the courts and the police.[32]

In his speeches, Chirac frequently used the term "insecurity." Because this term has different meanings for different people, insecurity became a coalition-building tool, bringing together different constituencies that shared only a general sense of anxiety.[33] Chirac appealed to these disparate groups, framing policing as a right-wing issue that Jospin and other left-wing politicians could not tackle or even understand because of their ideological blindness and their reluctance to flex the state's repressive muscles.[34] Like American President George W. Bush, who portrayed himself as the best guardian of national security after September 11, President Chirac exploited and amplified the prevailing sense of global collective insecurity. Moreover, like John Kerry during the 2004 American presidential campaign, Lionel Jospin found it difficult to win an ideological struggle over security issues.

Jacques Chirac was not the only candidate to benefit from the new collective obsession with insecurity. On the far right, Jean-Marie Le Pen claimed to be the only politician capable of restoring law and order; after all, more than Chirac, he had long denounced the negative effects of delinquency. In contrast to Le Pen's past presidential campaigns, during which he made scandalous remarks that attracted widespread negative media coverage, in 2002 he ran an oddly uneventful campaign that attracted little media attention.[35] While most pundits and journalists believed that this gentler style pointed to the political decline of Le Pen and the far right, he became a more acceptable electoral option for many disillusioned French electors. On the eve of the first ballot, few observers predicted that the debate over insecurity would benefit Le Pen's campaign.[36]

On April 21, the results of the first ballot stunned France: Chirac and Le Pen—not Jospin—made it to the second round. Le Pen, long viewed as an extremist, would have the opportunity to run alone against the incumbent president. Realizing that the political and media obsession with insecurity may have favored Le Pen, observers immediately blamed journalists and media outlets for tabloid-style coverage of crime and delinquency. Reacting to these accusations, television stations modified the content of the lately popular evening news, and crime coverage dropped dramatically between April 21 and May 5, the day of the second ballot.[37] Instead of focusing on crime and delinquency, journalists joined the national crusade against Le Pen, which took the form of massive street protests and public outrage over his presence in the second round of the presidential campaign.

Labeled as an enemy of the Republic, Le Pen suddenly became the center of political and media attention. From the fear of crime, the political and media debate moved to the fear of Le Pen and his xenophobic ideas:

> As the first round result effectively ended the election as a competitive battle, the only issue on the media's agenda was now Le Pen himself, with his personification of intolerance and xenophobia. Many outlets of the national and regional press were proactive in disseminating a strong anti-Le Pen message.[38]

Because surveys showed that Le Pen had no chance of winning against Chirac, the social and political mobilization against Le Pen was framed as a symbolic crusade aimed at restoring the image of a tolerant and open Republic. During the second round of the presidential campaign, Chirac found it easy to depict himself as the savior of the Republic against Le Pen. Many left-wing intellectuals and politicians explicitly supported Chirac to avoid the election of Le Pen. After all, many believed that the divisions of the left and the "protest vote" against Jospin favored the shocking outcome of the first ballot. Finally, Chirac won the second ballot with more than 80 percent of the popular vote.[39]

During the two last weeks of the presidential campaign, insecurity, the theme that helped both Chirac and Le Pen gain political ground during the first round, moved to the periphery of the political debate. But after the legislative elections of June 2002, Chirac and the new right-wing government of Jean-Pierre Raffarin enacted measures to toughen law enforcement and to put more police officers on the streets. The most debated new legislation dealing with insecurity was the "Sarkozy Law" (*Loi 2003–239 du 18 mars 2003 pour la sécurité intérieure*), which embodied the zero tolerance logic well known in the United States.[40] Most of the legislation was about creating new infractions and offenses related to "incivilities" and youth delinquency, while giving more power to law enforcement officers: for example, it cracked down on loitering, prostitution, organized or aggressive begging, and the harassment of civil servants and public employees. The "Sarkozy Law" also made it illegal to insult the French flag and national anthem. Left-wing politicians depicted the legislation as a repressive attack against the poor and launched legal actions against several potentially unconstitutional provisions.[41] The enactment of the "Sarkozy Law" shows how state protection can become repressive and can target deprived segments of the population.

Beyond the legislative arena, the minister in charge of policing, Nicolas Sarkozy, became the most popular figure of the Raffarin government. Often appearing on television, Sarkozy toured France visiting police stations to support the war on crime and delinquency. This campaign resulted directly from the 2002 presidential debate over insecurity, which had long-term political and policy consequences: it constructed the need to reform the French police and justice system in a comprehensive way. Long after the reelection of Chirac, the debate over the effectiveness and the moral legitimacy of the punitive approach to delinquency adopted in 2002 remained open. For some observers, the right-wing struggle against insecurity represented only a backlash against the poor and ethnic minorities; for others, it simply constituted a spectacular but ineffective way to deal with France's many social problems.[42] Though French policymakers did not fully embrace the American punitive model, which would have resulted in skyrocketing prison rates,[43] debates over security durably affected a significant aspect of state protection.

Discussion

As Charles Tilly's analysis reminds us, the modern state emerged in part as a source of protection against crime and violence. Issues of crime and violence are still a crucial component of the contemporary political debates in Western Europe and North America. This chapter explored the French debate on insecurity to stress the interplay of factors that pushed crime and delinquency to the center of the policy agenda before, during, and immediately after the 2002 presidential campaign.

The issues that came to the forefront of public consciousness in this election have affected current policy, leading to what some view as a repressive expansion of state protection in France. As we have seen, state protection is an ambiguous, potentially repressive reality rooted in threats that political leaders may amplify or downplay in order to promote their own agenda. From this angle, this case study shows that political leaders are dynamically involved in the construction of collective insecurity, which is not only about media-induced effects.

In France, the reduction of the meaning of "insecurity" to law-enforcement issues may construe physical security as the most legitimate form of state protection at the expense of others. As we discuss in this book's Conclusion, this could mean that, as in the United States after the events of September 11, right-wing politicians attempted to shift the public's attention from social and environmental protection to the forms of state intervention that are more attuned to their ideological and electoral goals.

This chapter further backs the arguments formulated in Chapter Four. First, the concept of moral panic only partially applies to the 2002 electoral episode. On the one hand, FN discourse on "organized ethnic bands" represented a clear attempt to transform members of ethnic minorities into "folk devils." Furthermore, police unions, journalists, and right-wing politicians clearly acted as moral entrepreneurs targeting a specific population described as dangerous—in this case, youth delinquents. But on the other hand, it was the election of Le Pen to the second round of the presidential election, *not* media reports on crime, that created a strong sense of national panic. Ironically, for the majority of the population, a powerful politician became the true "folk devil." The population's overwhelming rejection of Le Pen's campaign, and the absence of documented widespread popular panic about delinquency, explain why the concept of moral panic does not fully apply to this case.

Second, the 2002 episode seems consistent with the idea of increased risk perception in advanced industrial societies, as French citizens have become more and more concerned with crime and delinquency. In this particular case, however, the threat became so dramatized that such acute risk perception constituted at least as much a political and media construction as an assessment of the threat itself. Ironically, this is related to the threat infrastructure of urban delinquency, which allows for sudden waves of collective insecurity related to images of violence and chaos.

Third, both blame avoidance and credit claiming were central to the politics of this election. Both Chirac and Le Pen successfully claimed credit for addressing the issues of crime and delinquency while criticizing the apparent "inaction" of Jospin, who could not shield his party from blame emanating from the right.

Fourth, Jospin's inability to deflect blame effectively stemmed from the ideas and past policy decisions of his Socialist Party, whose heritage seemed at odds with the "repressive" turn in French politics. We see again that institutional features—in this case, features of the political party—create powerful constraints for strategic actors.

Finally, this case illustrates the differences between proactive and reactive behavior in the politics of insecurity. In this case, Jospin and his two main right-wing opponents employed different tactics. Chirac and Le Pen clearly adopted proactive strategies that pushed issues of crime and delinquency onto the agenda, and they constructed it as a serious threat to social order necessitating a major right-wing and punitive turn in French society. On the other hand, Jospin adopted a politically unsustainable reactive strategy, and as a result his campaign came to an early end.

The next chapter will look at two other presidential campaigns, this time in the United States.

Notes

1. Loïc Wacquant (1999), *Les Prisons de la misère* (Paris: Raisons d'agir/Le Seuil).

2. On this issue, see Éric Maurin (2004), *Le ghetto français: Enquête sur le séparatisme social* (Paris: Le Seuil).

3. Daniel Béland and Randall Hansen (2000), "Reforming the French Welfare State: Solidarity, Social Exclusion and the Three Crises of Citizenship," *West European Politics* 23(1): 47–64.

   On the French debate about social exclusion, see Alban Goguel d'Allondans (2003), *L'exclusion sociale: les métamorphoses d'un concept (1960–2000)*(Paris: L'Harmattan), and Hilary Silver (1994), "Social Exclusion and Social Solidarity: Three Paradigms," *International Labour Review* 133(5–6): 531–78.

4. On this issue, see Dominique Schnapper (1998), *Community of Citizens: On the Modern Idea of Nationality* (New Brunswick: Transaction).

5. The large presence of people from North African background is related to colonial legacies, as Algeria, Morocco, and Tunis freed themselves from French domination only in the postwar era.

6. Some commentators believe that secularism has become an obstacle to the integration of immigrants and citizens of North African background. On this issue, see Jane Freedman (2004), "Secularism as a Barrier to Integration? The French Dilemma," *International Migration* 42(2): 5–27.

7. Steven Griggs (2004), "Jacques Chirac's Campaign: President in Spite of Himself?" in John Gaffney, ed., *The French Presidential and Legislative Elections of 2002* (Aldershot: Ashgate Publishing), pp. 132–148.

8. Peter Davies (1999), *The Front National in France: Ideology, Discourse and Power* (London: Routledge), p. 45.

9. Ibid., pp. 158–59.

10. Jens Rydgren (2004), *The Populist Challenge: Political Protest and Ethnonationalist Mobilization in France* (New York: Berghahn Books), p. 76.

11. Ibid., p. 186.

12. For a discussion of the emergence of the *Front national* during the 1980s and early 1990s, see Nonna Mayer and Pascal Perrineau, eds. (1996), *Le Front National à découvert* (Paris: La Découverte).

13. Laurent Mucchielli (2002), "Misère du débat sur 'l'insécurité'," *Journal du droit des jeunes* 217: 16–19.

   Despite their limitations, there is probably some truth to these statistics. See Hugues Lagrange (2004), *Demandes de sécurité: France, Europe, Etats-Unis* (Paris: La République des idées/Le Seuil).

14. For example, two authors referred to the "available data" to support the claim that "since 1982, crime has taken root in hundreds of urban and suburban neighborhoods in France. "Alain Bauer and Xavier Raufer (1998), *Violences et insécurités urbaines* (Paris: Presses Universitaires de France), p. 5.

    A closer examination of the data points to a more complex situation: see Laurent Mucchielli (1999), *Expertise ou supercherie sur les "violences urbaines"?* (available online at laurent.mucchielli.free.fr [accessed March 2007]).

15. In France, the unemployment rate reached a record level of 12.6 percent in June 1997. By March 2001, it had fallen to 8.7 percent, the same as its level in the early 1980s. Jean Pisani-Ferry (2001), *Employment in France* (Paris: Premier Ministre—Services d'information du gouvernement), June.

16. Philippe Robert (2002), "Le sentiment d'insécurité" in Laurent Mucchielli and Philippe Robert, *Crime et sécurité: l'état des savoirs* (Paris: La Découverte), pp. 367–75.

17. Julien Terral (2004), *L'insécurité au journal télévisé: La campagne présidentielle de 2002* (Paris: L'Harmattan), p. 31.

18. "The number of private security personnel rose from 11,500 in 1983 to 94,000 in 1998, and is probably 130,000 today." See Jacques de Maillard and Sébastian Roché (2004), "Crime and Justice in France: Time Trends, Policies and Political Debate," *European Journal of Criminology* 1(1): 111–51. This article offers an overview of recent French scholarly literature on crime and insecurity.

19. Lionel Jospin (1997), *Des villes sûres pour des citoyens libres: allocution de Monsieur Lionel Jospin, Premier Ministre, au Colloque de Villepinte, le samedi 25 octobre 1997* (Paris: Office of the French Prime Minister).

20. Members of the Socialist Party belong mostly to the middle class, and they seldom support the conservative push for strict law enforcement. The Communist Party could adopt a tougher stance on crime because its working-class constituency is more receptive to that type of approach. See Henri Rey (2002), "La sécurité dans le debate," in Laurent Mucchielli and Philippe Robert, eds., *Crime et sécurité: l'état des savoirs* (Paris: La Découverte), pp. 25–32.

21. Jacques Chirac (1998), *Voeux aux français* (Paris: Palais de l'Elysée), December 31.

22. Jacques Chirac (2001), *Interview télévisée à l'occasion de la fête nationale* (Paris: Palais de l'Elysée), July 14.

23. Jacques Gerstlé (2003), "Une fenêtre d'opportunité électorale," in Pascal Perrineau and Colette Ysmal, eds., *Le vote de tous les refus: les*

élections présidentielle et législatives de 2002 (Paris: Presses de Sciences Po), pp. 29–52.

24. Catherine Gorgeon and Dominique Monjardet (2002), *Le malaise policier, Regards sur l'actualité 279* (Paris: La documentation française), March.

25. Terral, *L'insécurité au journal télévisé*, p. 32. The French police also participated in the political construction of insecurity through the publication of reports about delinquency and criminality in France: Laurent Mucchielli (2001), "L'expertise policière des 'violences urbaines,'" *Informations sociales* 92: 14–23.

26. Alistair Cole (2002), "A Strange Affair: The 2002 Presidential and Parliamentary Elections in France," *Government and Opposition* 37(3): 317–42.

27. Gerstlé, "Une fenêtre d'opportunité électorale," p. 35.

28. Ben Clift (2004), "Lionel Jospin's Campaign and the Socialist Left: The 'Earthquake' and its Aftershocks" in John Gaffney, ed., *The French Presidential and Legislative Elections of 2002* (Aldershot: Ashgate), pp. 149–68.

29. Ibid.

30. Terral, *L'insécurité au journal télévisé*.

31. Ibid.

32. Griggs, "Jacques Chirac's Campaign," p. 138.

33. Ibid.

34. In his last speech before the end of the first round, the President accused Jospin of doing little more than talk about insecurity. Jacques Chirac (2002), *Discours de Monsieur Jacques Chirac à Lille* (Paris: Palais de l'Elysée), April 18.

35. Cole, "A Strange Affair," p. 324.

36. Catherine Fieschi (2004), "Jean-Marie Le Pen and the Front National: Crisis and Recovery" in John Gaffney, ed., *The French Presidential and Legislative Elections of 2002* (Aldershot: Ashgate), pp. 169–84.

37. In his book, Terral mentions a 77-percent decrease in the time devoted to crime-related issues during the evening news on the three main French television stations: *L'insécurité au journal televise*, p. 61.

38. Raymond Kuhn (2004), "The Media and the Elections" in John Gaffney, ed., *The French Presidential and Legislative Elections of 2002* (Aldershot: Ashgate), pp. 83–116 (98).

39. Cole, "A Strange Affair."

40. Wacquant, *Les prisons de la misère*.

41. *Le Monde* (special section) (2003), "Sécurité: les interdits de la loi Sarkozy," February 14. These legal actions later proved unsuccessful.

42. On this debate, see Robert Castel (2003), *L'insécurité sociale: Qu'est-ce qu'être protégé?* (Paris: La République des idées/Le Seuil). Dramatic large-scale riots in fall 2005 may have stressed the shortcomings of the punitive approach adopted in the aftermath of the 2002 presidential election. These riots represented the "worst unrest since the student uprisings of 1968." Associated Press (2005), "France Declares State of Emergency," *New York Times*, November 9.

    Pointing to profound ethnic conflicts and a revolt against police harassment, such riots embarrassed Nicolas Sarkozy, who was accused of aggravating tensions with his defiant attitude towards suburban delinquents. See Jean-Baptiste de Montvalon (2005), "Émeutes de Clichy-sous-Bois: les interventions de Nicolas Sarkozy sont contestées, même à droite," *Le Monde*, November 1.

43. In March 2004, France's prison population rate was 95 per 100,000 residents, as compared to 714 in the United States. France's rate is similar to Germany's and lower than the United Kingdom's. See International Centre for Prison Studies (2004), *World Prison Brief* (available online at www.kcl.ac.uk/depsta/rel/icps/worldbrief/world_brief.html [accessed March 2007]).

Without Health Coverage

Technological, demographic, and economic transformations in recent decades have contributed to a sharp increase in medical costs. Partly for this reason, access to health insurance coverage has become a central political issue for citizens in advanced industrial societies. Debates over the potentially negative impact of economic globalization on social policy development, which has sparked concerns about the future of healthcare, crosses national borders. But the debate over health insurance coverage is unique to the United States, which remains the only advanced industrial country in which health insurance does not cover the whole population.[1] This situation illustrates the absence of comprehensive social citizenship in the United States.[2] In the field of social policy, the United States has not developed state protection to the level of countries such as France, Germany, and Sweden. Even strong free-market countries like Britain and Canada provide all citizens with health insurance coverage.[3]

This chapter looks at the politics of health insurance coverage in the United States during the 1990s and early 2000s, with a focus on President Clinton's Health Security initiative and the healthcare debate during the 2004 presidential campaign. As we will see, Americans have fairly accurate perceptions of the risk of losing their health insurance; most deal with health insurance problems in everyday life, which is not the case for terrorism or violent crime. Despite a threat infrastructure characterized by slow-moving structural forces, media stories and political discourse help transform personal health insurance problems into a pressing social and political issue. However, debate on healthcare reform is hardly a source of panic, regardless of potentially swift fluctuations in the policy agenda. This absence of panic waves is related to the particular threat infrastructure of health insecurity.

Health insurance was a major issue in the 1992 presidential election, and it reemerged on the federal agenda during the 2004 campaign. Candidate John Kerry, like Bill Clinton before him, constructed health coverage as a middle-class issue while downplaying the role of the federal state in his healthcare proposal. As opposed to the situation prevailing in aviation security after September 11, 2001, powerful economic interests opposed the enactment of comprehensive reform, and no sense of national crisis and radical insecurity affecting the whole population supported the need to deeply alter the existing balance between the public and private sectors.

Health Insurance and Insecurity: A Historical Perspective

In 1883, Germany became the first country to introduce a public health insurance scheme. At first, their "sickness fund" offered only limited coverage to industrial workers. In the early twentieth century, other countries adopted relatively modest public health insurance programs; in 1911, for example, the British government enacted a national health insurance system that targeted manual workers. As in Germany, the rationale of public health insurance was to help low-income workers bear the cost of healthcare.[4] During the 1910s, politicians in the United States debated public health insurance, but opposition from doctors and business interests in the context of fiscal federalism prevented the establishment of public health insurance schemes at the state level. Furthermore, many citizens and elected officials associated health insurance with Germany, which worked to the measure's disadvantage as World War I approached.[5]

During the 1930s, other industrial countries like New Zealand enacted public health insurance schemes for workers and their families to reduce economic insecurity related to high medical costs and restricted private insurance coverage.[6] At the time, health insurance received consideration in the United States as well. During the New Deal, the administration of President Franklin Roosevelt decided not to include health insurance in the Social Security Act of 1935 for two strategic reasons. First, the mobilization of the powerful American Medical Association could have derailed the enactment of this omnibus legislation, which already included provisions about old-age insurance, unemployment insurance, and social assistance for mothers and the elderly. Postponing the enactment of public health insurance thus seemed necessary to facilitate adoption of the Social Security Act. Second, healthcare costs were not a crucial social and economic concern during the Great Depression; in 1935, widespread unemployment and, to a lesser extent, old-age insecurity were the most pressing social issues of the day.[7]

Efforts to enact national health insurance in the late 1930s failed, and in the following decade private health benefits underwent massive expansion, reducing the perceived need for national health insurance. By the late 1940s, when President Truman promoted national health insurance as part of the Fair Deal, the enthusiasm of workers and labor officials for that policy alternative had faded. Vested interests in the private medical sector, mainly private insurance companies, mobilized to prevent the enactment of this measure. As a result, the only significant health-related legislation Congress enacted at the time focused on health research and on hospital construction.[8] Meanwhile, most advanced industrial countries had enacted public health insurance schemes in which the level of coverage increased over time. In the postwar era, countries like Britain, Canada, and Sweden all enacted universal, national health insurance.[9]

In the United States, the large Democratic majority in Congress elected in the aftermath of President John F. Kennedy's assassination favored the enactment of Medicare, which covered old-age insurance beneficiaries, and Medicaid, which covered public assistance beneficiaries, in 1965. During the 1960s, an implicit division of labor between the state and the private insurance sector emerged: the former would cover the most vulnerable citizens, seldom covered by private insurance—i.e., the "bad risks"—while the latter would cover the rest of the population.[10] The effort to cover vulnerable citizens reduced the apparent need for universal public health insurance for the entire population. In the 1970s and 1980s, campaigns to enact a national health insurance scheme failed in part because of that situation, and in part because rising costs made any debate of national health insurance difficult. Vested interests in the private medical sector, such as private insurance companies, opposed the enactment of national health insurance, arguing that the division of labor between the state and the private sector worked well. Facing these strong obstacles, reformers succeeded only at increasing Medicare and Medicaid coverage. Over the last two decades, for example, Medicaid expanded from a program that covered only people on social assistance to one that covered most children and some adult workers living in poverty.[11]

In the early 1990s, the number of uninsured—more than 35 million—indicated a significant social problem that now reemerges cyclically on the policy agenda. With medical costs rising, the uninsured face economic insecurity; a long stay at the hospital could result in enormous personal debts. Gaps in health insurance coverage have created public health concerns because uninsured individuals are less likely to make choices compatible with preventive medicine. Furthermore, the prospect of losing one's health coverage represents a significant source of insecurity: for millions of Americans, becoming unemployed means losing health coverage.[12]

The uninsured have not necessarily lost insurance; some of them were never insured in the first place. Many of these individuals had low-paying jobs without health coverage, and still others had chosen not to purchase coverage offered by employers because of the expense. However, in the United States, being uninsured is not an absolute barrier to the receipt of medical care. Many hospitals treat uninsured individuals and, when unable to place them on Medicaid, hospital administrators write off the visits as bad debt or as charity. The uninsured in need of urgent care frequently use emergency rooms for medical care, but whether they receive the same quality of treatment as insured individuals remains an open question. Most citizens assume that the uninsured lag behind in preventive care, and, if they are admitted to hospitals, receive a lower level of care.[13]

In the United States, economic insecurity from unemployment and the lack of health insurance coverage are concretely related. Americans' expectations about future employment and health coverage status are consistent with subsequent realizations. That is, if individuals have excessively pessimistic views on their chances of becoming a crime victim, for example, their perception of socioeconomic risks like unemployment and being uninsured is on average very accurate. Males and females aged eighteen to thirty-four face the highest risk of losing health insurance coverage over the next twelve months in any given period. The level of economic insecurity related to the absence of health coverage is higher among African Americans and those with no post-secondary education. The threat infrastructure of health insecurity suggests that economic insecurity is highly stratified according to factors like age, education, and race/ethnicity.[14]

Health Coverage and Middle Class Insecurity: The Clinton Plan

Although these problems have long existed, the large number of people without health insurance increased significantly in the early 1990s. Between 1988 and 1993, the number of uninsured rose from 33.7 to 40.9 million, an increase from 13 percent to more than 15 percent of the American population.[15] Higher unemployment and employers' attempts to reduce costs partly explained this decline in health coverage. Simultaneously, health-care costs soared; consuming more than 15 percent of the gross domestic product (GDP), healthcare costs increased far more rapidly than the rate of inflation. Between 1980 and 1993, for example, the rate of inflation increased by 71 percent, while healthcare costs increased by almost 200 percent. These numbers point to a paradox: "The United States spends substantially more on healthcare than any other nation, despite the fact that this country is the only advanced democracy with a significant share of its population uninsured."[16] Knowledge of this paradox may have aggravated popular dissatisfaction towards the American healthcare system in the early 1990s.

Rising costs and declining coverage moved the issue of health insurance coverage onto the federal policy agenda on the eve of the 1992 presidential campaign. During the 1980s, the mass media had seldom addressed healthcare reform, but in the early 1990s the number of stories about this issue featured in the three largest national newspapers, the *Christian Science Monitor, New York Times,* and *Wall Street Journal,* increased dramatically:

> [T]he total number of articles rose slightly in the latter half of the 1980s, but the real jump took place in 1991, as the number of articles grew from five to thirty-five, only to be followed by another more dramatic rise in 1992 as the number of articles reached ninety-three.[17]

These reports made citizens more aware of the scope of American healthcare financing and coverage problems, and support for comprehensive healthcare reform increased in the early 1990s. The idea that the private sector could guarantee the health insurance coverage of all workers seemed to fade in an era of downsizing and cost-containment. The very nature of the economic downturn that started in 1989 and worsened through 1991 exacerbated popular discontent toward the American healthcare system:

> By promoting a sense of economic insecurity, the recession heightened public anxiety about the escalating cost of medical care and the fragility of employer-sponsored health insurance. Moreover, the recession was harder on white-collar and professional workers than were other recent economic downturns, forcing middle income Americans who had taken their personal healthcare arrangements for granted to face the prospect of losing their health insurance or having their coverage cut back. [According to public opinion data,] all the factors associated with economic slumps—unemployment, disenchantment with the business community, and economic anxiety—increased public support for government involvement in healthcare. . . . [18]

Though many individuals can fall back on unemployment compensation for a limited period, economic downturns increase collective insecurity. In turn, this situation promotes the expansion of state protection in the field of healthcare as in other social policy areas. But, as we will see below, in the absence of a strong sense of national crisis, powerful vested interests are in a strong position to prevent the expansion of state protection in the context of checks and balances.

During the 1992 campaign, Democratic candidate Bill Clinton criticized the administration of George H. W. Bush for doing too little to increase health coverage and to fight economic insecurity, and Clinton proposed an ambitious healthcare proposal that would solve these problems. During the campaign, however, Clinton's reform plan remained vague in part because, in the United States, healthcare reform is one of the riskiest tasks federal officials can undertake. A vague plan could help Clinton avoid political backlash during the campaign, because powerful interests could not attack a plan that provided few policy details.

Aware of the powerful interests that are tied to private hospitals and insurance companies, Clinton explicitly rejected single-payer, national health insurance. This decision represented a sharp departure from traditional Democratic proposals. Furthermore, Clinton pledged that his proposed regulatory system would not require new federal taxes: employers would bear the costs of extended coverage. His discourse targeted members of the middle class afraid of losing their health insurance. Using concrete, personal examples, Clinton talked about families unable to keep their health insurance "just at the moment when their own illness or those of family members required it."[19]

In his acceptance speech to the Democratic National Convention, Clinton promised an America in which "healthcare is a right, not a privilege, in which we say to all of our people: Your government has the courage finally to take on the healthcare profiteers and make healthcare affordable for every family."[20] Focusing on middle-class insecurity enabled the Democratic candidate to connect with the electorate without looking like a "liberal" interested mainly in the fate of the poor and minorities. For Clinton, framing health coverage as a middle-class issue thus represented a blame avoidance strategy, as well as a way to address the concerns of the majority of voters.[21]

Moreover, as the two above quotes suggest, Clinton focused extensively on "family values" and the idea that the lack of private coverage affects not only workers but the rest of their family. According to Clinton, private insurance schemes failed to protect many American families and, for that reason, the federal state had to step in to help those in need. Clinton's apparent commitment to "family values," a concept that had long been associated with the conservative Republican camp, constituted another blame avoidance exercise.

To further neutralize traditional Republican attacks involving the "L word"—liberalism—Clinton adopted a tough stance on welfare reform. His proposal for welfare, as with healthcare, became part of a new Democratic agenda. The ideologically ambiguous nature of this agenda made it more difficult for President Bush to attack it. In November 1992, Clinton defeated Bush, who was blamed during the campaign for not responding adequately to recession in the early 1990s.[22]

As before his election, Clinton promoted "managed competition" as an imaginative tool that would simultaneously extend health insurance coverage and control the increase in medical costs while preserving the market-oriented nature of the American healthcare system. Managed competition would solve the two most crucial problems of the American healthcare system without paving the way to "socialized medicine." This attempt to solve traditional policy problems using new methods not defined as "liberal" or "conservative," a strategic effort to shield the Clinton Administration and the Democratic Party against potential attacks from Republican and business circles, constituted the quintessential New Democrat approach to social policy.[23]

For the new president, fighting insecurity and reducing costs without explicitly attacking the vested interests attached to the private healthcare system seemed the only viable strategy to adopt comprehensive healthcare reform in the context of divided government. Furthermore, he stressed the need to maintain high-quality care while extending health insurance coverage. In his first State of the Union address, Clinton stated:

> We will provide security to all our families, so that no one will be denied the coverage they need. We will root out fraud and outrageous charges, and make sure that paperwork no longer chokes you or your doctor. And we will maintain American standards—the highest quality medical care in the world and the choices we demand and deserve. The American people expect us to deal with healthcare. And we must deal with it now.[24]

This speech outlined many of the President's complex reform goals; combating economic insecurity through the extension of health insurance coverage was only one policy goal among others.

Although the president established a healthcare task force not long after taking office, his plan was announced only in September 1993, so the plan was debated after the traditional "honeymoon period" between Congress and new presidents.[25] The most obvious political problem with the president's healthcare proposal was its complexity. His so-called Health Security Bill represented a complicated set of regulatory agencies and mechanisms that most citizens, and even some policy experts, could not grasp. In all policy areas, complex ideas and proposals are difficult to sell to the public, and the president first attempted to hide this complexity while downplaying the role of the federal state in his legislative proposal.

In a speech to a joint session of Congress in September 1993, the president did not mention the complex regulatory rules contained in his Health Security plan. Instead, he stressed the insecurity caused by the lack of health insurance coverage:

> Millions of Americans are just a pink slip away from losing their health insurance and one serious illness away from losing all their savings. Millions more are locked into the jobs they have now just because they or someone in their family has once been sick and they have what is called the preexisting condition. And on any given day, over 37 million Americans, most of them working people and their little children, have no health insurance at all.[26]

Focusing on the growing health-related insecurity affecting the middle class, Clinton downplayed the bureaucracy of the bill in order to avoid blame from conservative ranks. Moreover, he did not even mention the network of health alliances at the center of such a legislative proposal. These health alliances would constitute regional agencies that regrouped all consumers of health insurance (i.e., individuals, firms, and public agencies); some of these agencies would then act as purchasing agents for the population as a whole. Downplaying the role of the federal state in the proposed reform model, Clinton attempted to depict it as a uniquely American, market-oriented solution to specifically American problems.[27]

As a blame avoidance strategy, this attempt to downplay the role of the federal state was meant to reassure the population and powerful interest groups involved in health politics. The idea of managed competition itself featured an explicit acknowledgment of the private sector's central role in the American healthcare system. In opposition to the "single-payer" model, "managed competition" involved the regulation of private health insurance schemes, not their replacement by a national, public health insurance system. Depicting Health Security as a moderate policy alternative, the president focused less on universal health insurance coverage than on how his proposal would preserve "consumer choice." In general, the Clinton Administration addressed the concerns of middle-class citizens who were afraid of losing their health insurance but who wanted to preserve their ability to choose their own doctor and healthcare plan—a reality that points to the tradeoffs between personal freedom and state protection discussed in Chapter One.

Over time, the idea of covering the 37 million American citizens without health insurance became less central to the administration's rhetoric, despite the economic belief that the uninsured were driving up insurance premiums for the middle class.[28] The insecurity of middle-class citizens who were already insured but afraid of losing their apparent freedom to choose paradoxically seemed more significant politically than the insecurity of millions of poorer workers who lived without health insurance. Of course, poorer citizens have a far lower rate of electoral participation than the middle class and the wealthy;[29] without massive mobilization like that witnessed during the 1960s, the poor rarely have any significant impact on federal policymaking.[30]

Public interest in Clinton's plan gradually waned. Although President Clinton framed the Health Security bill as a market-based and pro-middle class policy alternative, Republican leaders depicted the Clinton plan as an overly complex proposal that would bring more big government and reduce personal freedom and consumer choice. Likewise, in addition to private insurance companies predictably opposing the plan, most large corporations, with the exception of the automobile industry, condemned it. The fiercest opposition came from organizations representing small businesses, such as the Chamber of Commerce and National Federation of Independent Business. Support for the Clinton plan declined sharply: in mid-September 1993, polls showed that a large majority of people supported the plan's principles, but six weeks later the public was already far more divided.[31] Finally, even the Democratic majority in Congress refused to seriously consider the Health Security Bill, which died long before the midterm elections of November 1994. The issue disappeared from the agenda; the defeat of the Health Security Bill crushed Clinton's political capital, and led to the sweeping victory of the Republican Party at the 1994 Congressional elections.

To sell this legislation to the public and to avoid conservative attacks, the Clinton Administration focused more on middle-class individuals afraid of losing their health insurance than on the uninsured. This reflects a broader trend of contemporary American politics, in which less-advantaged citizens

> are so absent from discussions in Washington that federal officials are likely to hear about their concerns, if at all, from more privileged advocates who speak for the disadvantaged. Politicians hear most regularly about the concern of business and the most affluent.[32]

Furthermore, conservative officials had launched a campaign against social programs designed to help the poor. For example, conservatives argued for years that the existing Aid for Families with Dependent Children (AFDC) program undermined work ethics and traditional family values. Two years after the Health Security Bill failed, the Republican Congress adopted Temporary Aid for Needy Families (TANF), a new program that replaced AFDC while imposing workfare and strict time limits on most social assistance recipients. After vetoing it twice, Clinton finally signed this "punitive" legislation, which was much harsher than his initial welfare reform proposal.[33]

Health Insurance and Economic Security in the 2004 Presidential Campaign

Democrats took more than a decade to unveil another comprehensive proposal on health insurance coverage. Because of the backlash against big government that followed the legislative failure of the Health Security Bill, Democrats could not introduce a new comprehensive reform package for the remainder of the Clinton Administration. Instead, they supported more modest health initiatives dealing with drug coverage, Medicaid, and Medicare reform. During the 2000 presidential campaign, Vice President and Democratic presidential candidate Al Gore did not propose bold health care changes in part because he wanted to distinguish himself from President Clinton, who had placed health coverage at the center of his first presidential campaign.

The lack of ambitious federal health coverage proposals after 1994 did not stem from a major improvement in the status of the uninsured. Although economic prosperity and low unemployment favored a slight decline in the percentage of uninsured, from 17 percent of the population in 1998 to 15.8 percent in 2000, such modest improvement, as well as economic prosperity, seemed to reduce the need to restructure the healthcare system.[34] The fact that health coverage moved to the periphery of the federal policy agenda for a decade after the defeat of Clinton's plan emphasizes the loose relationship between lasting protection needs and the agenda setting process, in which political leaders and their electoral strategies are crucial. A sense of collective insecurity on a specific problem does not keep this problem on the agenda in the absence of political leaders willing to address it openly, especially when powerful interests oppose comprehensive reform.

The economic recession of the early 2000s pushed health insurance coverage to the forefront of the 2004 presidential campaign.[35] As unemployment rose and businesses cut benefits to their employees, employment-based health insurance covered a decreasing portion of the population.[36] Soaring premiums and drug costs increased middle class dissatisfaction toward the healthcare system, and media reports on health insurance coverage and increasing premiums increased in frequency.[37] Because Democrats are traditionally associated with progressive healthcare reform, growing public and media concerns about health insurance created political opportunity for Democratic presidential candidate John Kerry. To seize this opportunity, Kerry launched a comprehensive healthcare proposal legitimized in relation to increasing health costs:

> Over the last three years, family premiums have increased by more than $2,600 and prescription drug prices have grown four times faster than infla-tion. These skyrocketing costs have hurt our economy and forced many fam-ilies into bankruptcy.[38]

Less comprehensive than the 1993 Health Security proposal, Kerry's plan aimed to lower family health insurance premiums while extending "af-fordable, high-quality coverage to 95 percent of Americans, including every child."[39] Although vague, this plan became one of the most debated pol-icy items of the Kerry campaign.

Although national security dominated the 2004 campaign, televised de-bates between Kerry and President George W. Bush prominently featured the issue of healthcare reform. During the third debate, Senator Kerry ex-plained the rationale for his plan. Like President Clinton more than a decade earlier, Kerry rejected single-payer, national health insurance; and like Clinton, he downplayed the role that the federal state would play in healthcare reform:[40]

> The fact is that my healthcare plan, America, is very simple. It gives you the choice. I don't force you to do anything. It's not a government plan. The government doesn't require you to do anything. You choose your doctor. You choose your plan.[41]

Kerry, as Clinton a decade earlier, framed health insurance coverage as a middle-class issue. His message targeted middle-class individuals con-cerned about soaring healthcare costs but afraid of losing their apparent freedom of choice and the services they have access to under the current healthcare system. In political discourse, the idea of the middle class is vague, and a large number of citizens identify with this category. This is why, like many other federal politicians, Kerry framed himself as "fight-ing for the middle class."[42]

During the second televised presidential debate, the Democratic candi-date accused President Bush of siding with drug companies and private in-surers instead of defending the interests of the middle class. To a certain extent, Kerry even blamed the president for the increase in the number of uninsured citizens witnessed during his first term—showing again how elected officials may be blamed for forms of collective insecurity for which they are not directly responsible.

In response, Bush claimed that Kerry's plan would cost as much as 1.5 tril-lion dollars, forcing new tax hikes that would crush the middle class. He also warned that under Kerry's plan federal civil servants would make crucial health-care decisions that users make under the current system—arguments similar to those Republicans used against the Health Security Bill a decade earlier.

Thus, both candidates used fear and insecurity to promote their policy alternatives: on one hand, Kerry referred to the growing insecurity of work-ers and families fearing the loss of health coverage, and on the other, Bush defended the current healthcare system, arguing that greater federal intervention could weaken both personal freedom and the quality of care currently available to those who have coverage.[43] The president's own plan to strengthen health coverage and help citizens cope with increasing premiums relied essentially on multiplying health savings accounts, enacting tax credits to maintain insurance coverage for laid-off workers, and making health insurance more affordable. But according to the Kaiser Family Foundation, this plan would reduce the number of uninsured by only 1.8 million;[44] considering that about 45 million American citizens were uninsured at the time, this figure seemed extremely modest. Furthermore, most of the $90 billion in tax credits "would actually help the rich, who need no help, and would be little help to the low-paid, who pay little or no tax and are most at risk of losing insurance."[45] From this point of view, the president's plan seemed less concerned than Kerry's with the health-related economic insecurity affecting the poor.

The 2004 debate over healthcare reform may not seem explicitly related to the issue of globalization, but during his campaign Kerry often stated that the federal state should prevent the overseas relocation of American jobs through new tax regulations. More important, Kerry's strategy to "keep high-paying jobs in America" included the reduction of healthcare costs, increasingly perceived as a major obstacle to the global competitiveness of American firms.[46] The debate over economic insecurity in the United States prominently features the issue of globalization, even when that topic is not explicitly mentioned. Even when healthcare is concerned, globalization is a major part of the discourse on collective insecurity in the United States.

The reelection of President Bush in November 2004 effectively killed the Kerry plan while further reducing the prospect of a major restructuring of the American healthcare system. Yet, as the abovementioned defeat of Clinton's Health Security bill suggests, the presence in the White House of a president committed to universal health coverage would not necessarily have paved the way to bold reforms in this policy area. In addition to divided government, entrenched vested interests in the American healthcare system further complicate the prospect for comprehensive reform.

Discussion

As with unemployment, the risk of becoming uninsured is grounded in the everyday experience of citizens and, because of this specific threat infrastructure, politicians cannot downplay or negate the insecurity associated with this risk. As opposed to the prevailing situation in fields of policing and national security, left-leaning politicians are in a better position to address concerns about economic insecurity and health insurance coverage. In the United States, Democrats have a clear advantage when these issues move onto the policy agenda, generally in a context of economic downturn and disillusion with private protection. However, such factors are not necessarily sufficient to guarantee the enactment of comprehensive reforms that may challenge powerful vested interests. Historically, only catastrophic events such as the Great Depression have paved the way for major expansions of federal social policy. A major transformation of the American health insurance system may not occur without the emergence of a broadly shared sense of emergency and national crisis that favors left-wing forces.[47]

In the early 1990s and during the 2004 presidential campaign, political candidates primarily addressed the insecurity of middle-class citizens, not of poorer citizens living without health insurance. American politicians are aware that addressing the economic insecurity of the middle class carries more political weight than addressing the economic insecurity of the working poor. As in other countries, there is a clear relationship between social inequalities and the politics of insecurity surrounding social policy issues. Often, politicians focus on forms of collective insecurity affecting those who are in a better position to mobilize politically. This is related to the electoral strategies of politicians. Collective insecurity and state protection have strong strategic meaning for them.

The development of social citizenship has faced formidable obstacles in the United States. Increasing collective insecurity does not always lead to an expansion of state protection. Although this chapter's case study shows how political leaders play a central role in the construction of insecurity, it constitutes a "negative case" as far as the potential causal link between collective insecurity and the expansion of state protection is concerned. As suggested, the reproduction of powerful vested interests in the private sector largely explains this outcome.[48]

To conclude this analysis, we return to the five claims formulated in Chapter Four. First, this chapter shows once again the limitations of the concept of moral panic. The threat infrastructure of health insurance policy is not based on sporadic episodes of collective insecurity. The concept of moral panic does not apply here, even though the health agenda, like most of the policy agenda, is unstable over time and, under some circumstances, health insurance debates can take an explicitly moral overtone.[49]

Second, this analysis suggests that political leaders are blamed for "market failures" and other social problems for which they are not necessarily responsible. For example, though politicians are not directly accountable for the decline in private coverage, citizens and other political leaders may blame them for such a decline and turn to the state for protection.

Third, elected officials claim credit for responding adequately to the threat—in this case, the decline in private coverage—while attempting to avoid blame for their apparent inaction or from controversial aspects of their proposals. Fourth, this chapter offers a striking example of how vested interests related to existing public and private policy arrangements create powerful constraints for political leaders.

And finally, this chapter stresses the diversity of political strategies and the distinction between proactive and reactive behavior in the political shaping of collective insecurity. On one hand, Clinton and Kerry participated actively in the construction of health insecurity as a pressing policy issue, as part of their party's ideological profile. On the other hand, President Bush, at least during the 2004 campaign, adopted a more reactive approach, partially because his administration had little interest in addressing this issue because of their pro-market agenda. In such a context, focusing proactively on terrorism represented a more appealing electoral strategy for Republicans.

In the aftermath of the 2005 Hurricane Katrina disaster, a new debate on economic insecurity and the lacunas of American state protection emerged to haunt President Bush and his allies, barely ten months after his reelection.[50] Despite the revitalized national focus on economic and racial inequities, however, the president did not call for major new social programs to fight these problems. Instead, in a televised speech, he praised the mobilization of charitable organizations like the Salvation Army before stating that the federal state should simply distribute federal land to low-income citizens who

> would pledge to build on the lot, with either a mortgage or help from a charitable organization like Habitat for Humanity. Home ownership is one of the great strengths of any community, and it must be a central part of our vision for the revival of this region.[51]

Although the federal state allocated more than 100 billion dollars to post-Katrina reconstruction, the New Orleans catastrophe did not trigger a new debate on social programs like universal health coverage, which could greatly increase the economic security of deprived segments of the American population.

Conclusion to Part II

The four case studies show the many facets of state protection and illustrate how the politics of insecurity is manifested through electoral and political strategies. As argued, political leaders and other officials play a significant role in the construction of collective insecurity. Facing a changing economic and political context, these actors are forced to modify their discourse and strategies while taking into account existing social inequalities and vested interests.

Political leaders can affect the content of media reports and the perception of older and newer threats. For example, the discourse of Jacques Chirac in the months preceding the 2002 French presidential election stimulated the multiplication of dramatic media reports about crime and delinquency. Political leaders do not only respond to media reports; they also proactively shape media representations of insecurity through their discourse and actions. Furthermore, media outlets can become a political and even partisan force that serve the strategic interests of a specific party or elected official.

That said, the four cases we have discussed are not purely political or media constructions. Collective insecurity is usually grounded in genuine threats or at least empirical facts that provide a starting point for the actors involved in the politics of insecurity. For example, though BSE did not kill as many people as early media reports speculated it would, it is a genuine health hazard. The March 1996 episode in Britain reflects the acute risk awareness present in advanced industrial societies. Additionally, paying close attention to the threat infrastructure of a particular policy area helps us to understand the constraints and opportunities political leaders face when they participate in the construction of collective insecurity.

Finally, globalization has become a potential source of collective insecurity in advanced industrial societies. Although globalization has not favored a sharp decline in the protective power of the state, discourse on and the concrete trends associated with globalization can significantly affect the politics of insecurity.

Notes

1. See Philip J. Funigiello (2005), *Chronic Politics: Health Care Security from FDR to George W. Bush* (Lawrence: University Press of Kansas); Colin Gordon (2003), *Dead on Arrival: The Politics of Health Care in Twentieth-Century America* (Princeton: Princeton University Press); Marie Gottschalk (2000), *The Shadow Welfare State: Labor, Business, and the Politics of Health Care in the United States* (Ithaca: Cornell University Press); Antonia Maioni (1998), *Parting at the Crossroads: The Emergence of Health Insurance in the United States and Canada* (Princeton: Princeton University Press); Rick Mayes (2005), *Universal Coverage: The Elusive Quest for National Health Insurance* (Ann Arbor: University of

Michigan Press); and Jill Quadagno (2005), *One Nation, Uninsured* (New York: Oxford University Press).

2. For a discussion on this issue, see Nancy Fraser and Linda Gordon (1992), "Contract versus Charity: Why Is There No Social Citizenship in the United States?" *Socialist Review* 22 (July): 45–68, and John Myles (1997), "Neither Rights Nor Contacts: The New Means Testing in U.S. Aging Policy" in Robert B. Hudson (ed.), *The Future of Age-Based Public Policy* (Baltimore: Johns Hopkins University Press), pp. 46–55.

3. Antonia Maioni (1998), *Parting at the Crossroads: The Emergence of Health Insurance in the United States and Canada* (Princeton: Princeton University Press); Jill Quadagno (2005), *One Nation, Uninsured* (New York, Oxford University Press).

4. On the origin of the 1911 reform, see Michael Freeden (1978), *The New Liberalism: An Ideology of Social Reform* (Oxford: Clarendon Press).

5. Ronald L. Numbers (1978), *Almost Persuaded: American Physicians and Compulsory Health Insurance, 1912–1920* (Baltimore: Johns Hopkins University Press).

6. On New Zealand, see Raymond Richards (1994), *Closing the Door to Destitution: The Shaping of the Social Security Acts of the United States and New Zealand* (University Park: Pennsylvania State University Press).

7. Edward D. Berkowitz (2000), "History and Social Security Reform," in Eric Kingson, Sheila Burke, and Uwe Reinhardt, eds., *Social Security and Medicare: Individual vs. Collective Risk and Responsibility* (Washington, DC: Brookings Institution), pp. 31–55.

8. Daniel Béland and Jacob S. Hacker (2004), "Ideas, Private Institutions, and American Welfare State 'Exceptionalism': The Case of Health and Old-Age Insurance in the United States, 1915–1965," *International Journal of Social Welfare* 13(1): 42–54.

9. For a historical and sociological perspective, see Mary Ruggie (1996), *Realignments in the Welfare State: Health Policy in the United States, Britain, and Canada* (New York: Columbia University Press), and Quadagno, *One Nation, Uninsured*.

10. Ruggie, *Realignments in the Welfare State*, pp. 147–50.

11. On this issue, see Lawrence D. Brown and Michael S. Sparer (2003), "Poor Program's Progress: The Unanticipated Politics of Medicaid Policy," *Health Affairs* 22(1): 31–44.

    In the early 1970s, Congress further expanded Medicare to cover beneficiaries of the federal disability insurance program.

12. See, for example, Jacob S. Hacker (1997), *The Road to Nowhere: The Genesis of President Clinton's Plan for Health Security* (Princeton: Princeton University Press), p. 19.

13. Most uninsured citizens are white, but non-elderly Hispanics and African-Americans have a greater chance of being uninsured. See

Quadagno, *One Nation, Uninsured*; John Geyman (2003), *Falling Through the Safety Net: Americans Without Health Insurance* (Monroe, ME: Common Courage Press); and Susan Starr Sered and Rushika Fernandopulle (2005), *Uninsured in America: Life and Death in the Land of Opportunity* (Berkeley: University of California Press).

Up-to-date information on the number and status of uninsured citizens in the United States is available on the Web site of the Center for Studying Health System Change (HSC): www.hschange.org (accessed March 2007).

14. Jeff Dominitz and Charles F. Manski (1997), "Perceptions of Economic Insecurity: Evidence from the Survey of Economic Expectations," *Public Opinion Quarterly* 61(2): 261–87.

15. Nicholas Laham (1996), *A Lost Cause: Bill Clinton's Campaign for National Health Insurance* (Westport, CT: Praeger), p. 22.

16. Ibid., p. 25.

17. Hacker, *The Road to Nowhere*, p. 21.

18. Ibid., p. 19.

19. Theda Skocpol (1996), *Boomerang: Health Care Reform and the Turn against Government* (New York: W. W. Norton), p. 45.

20. Clinton (1992), *Acceptance Speech to the Democratic National Convention*, New York (available online at www.4president.org/speeches/billclinton1992acceptance.htm [accessed March 2007]), July 16.

21. In the United States, electoral participation among the poor remains low. See Frances Fox Piven and Richard A. Cloward (2000), *Why Americans Still Don't Vote: And Why Politicians Want It That Way* (Boston: Beacon Press).

22. Daniel Béland, François Vergniolle de Chantal, and Alex Waddan (2002), "Third Way Social Policy: Clinton's Legacy?" *Policy and Politics* 30(1): 19–30.

23. Before Clinton took over the White House, "managed competition" was not the first choice of most Democrats for healthcare reform. See Frank R. Baumgartner and Jeffrey C. Talbert (1995), "From Setting a National Agenda on Health Care to Making Decisions in Congress," *Journal of Health Politics, Policy and Law* 20(2): 437–45.

24. Clinton (1993), *State of the Union Address* (Washington, DC: Office of the Press Secretary; available online at www.washingtonpost.com/wp-srv/politics/special/states/docs/sou93.htm [accessed March 2007]), February 17.

25. Haynes Johnson and David S. Broder (1997), *The System: The American Way of Politics at the Breaking Point* (Boston: Little, Brown), pp. 55–179.

26. Clinton (1993), *Address to a Joint Session of the Congress on Health Care Reform September 22*, in *Public Papers of the Presidents, William J.*

Clinton 1993, Vol. 2 (Washington, DC: U. S. Government Printing Office), pp. 1556–65.

27. Béland, Vergniolle de Chantal, and Waddan, "Third Way Social Policy."

28. Theda Skocpol (1992), *Health Care Reform and the Turn against Government* (New York: W. W. Norton), pp. 177–88.

29. American Political Science Association, Task Force on Inequality and American Democracy (2004), *American Democracy in the Age of Rising Inequality* (Washington, DC: American Political Science Association).

30. On this issue, see Frances Fox Piven and Richard Cloward (1971), *Regulating the Poor: The Functions of Public Welfare* (New York: Pantheon Books).

31. W. Schneider (1993), "A Fatal Flaw in Clinton's Health Plan," *National Journal*, November 6: 2696.

32. American Political Science Association (2004), *American Democracy in an Age of Rising Inequality*, cited in Jacob S. Hacker and Paul Pierson (2005), *Off Center: The Republican Revolution and the Erosion of American Democracy* (New Haven, CT: Yale University Press), p. 116.

33. R. Kent Weaver (2000), *Ending Welfare as We Know It* (Washington, DC: Brookings Institution).

   This outcome is related to the success of a conservative campaign that depicted AFDC as a program creating social problems rather than solving them; see Margaret Somers and Fred Block (2005), "From Poverty to Perversity: Ideational Embeddedness and the Rise and Reprise of Market Liberalism," *American Sociological Review* 70(2): 260–87.

34. State Coverage Initiatives (2004), "Who Are the Uninsured in the United States?" (available online at www.statecoverage.net/who.htm [accessed March 2007]).

35. For a general discussion about the 2004 presidential campaign, see William Crotty, ed., *A Defining Moment: The Presidential Election of 2004* (Armonk, NY: M. E. Sharpe), and Larry J. Sabato, ed. (2005), *Divided States of America: The Slash and Burn Politics of the 2004 Presidential Election* (New York: Longman).

   During the first term of George W. Bush, Congress enacted a drug plan for Medicare that does nothing to help Americans living without health insurance coverage. See Hacker and Pierson, *Off Center*, pp. 85–93.

36. United States Census Bureau (2004), *2003 Income, Poverty and Health Insurance (CPS Report) and Data from the American Community Survey (ACS)* (Washington, DC: Bureau of the Census), August 26.

37. See, for example, Paul Gores (2004), "Workers Pay Larger Share of Health Care Bill, Survey Says," *Milwaukee Journal Sentinel*, October 15.

38. JohnKerry.com (2004), "Senator John Kerry's Position on Issues Facing the American Public: Health Care" (available online at onthednc. bu.edu/issues/issues.htm [accessed March 2007]).

39. Ibid.

40. This does not mean that single-payer national health insurance is not debated in American policy circles. See David U. Himmelstein (2003), "National Health Insurance or Incremental Reform: Aim High, or at Our Feet," *American Journal of Public Health* 93(1), January: 102–05.

During the Democratic primaries, Representative Dennis J. Kucinich (Ohio) promoted national health insurance, an idea traditionally associated with Senator Ted Kennedy (Massachusetts) and the left wing of the Democratic Party. See, for example, David M. Halbfinger (2003), "Democrats Focus on Health Plans at Iowa Forum," *New York Times*, October 16: A25.

41. Commission on Presidential Debates (2004), *The Third Bush-Kerry Presidential Debate*, Tempe (available online at www.debates.org/pages/trans2004d.html [accessed March 2007]), October 13.

42. Commission on Presidential Debates (2004), *The Second Bush-Kerry Presidential Debate*, Saint Louis (available online at www.debates.org/pages/trans2004c.html [accessed March 2007]), October 8.

43. Bush-Cheney '04 Communications (2004), "The Kerry Line: John Kerry's Big Government Health Care Plan" (Washington, DC; available online at www.politicsla.com/press_releases/2004/October/101104_Kerry_line.pdf [accessed March 2007]), October 12.

44. Kaiser Family Foundation (2004), *Coverage and Cost Impacts of the President's Health Insurance Tax Credit and Tax Deduction Proposals* (Washington, DC: The Henry J. Kaiser Family Foundation; available online at www.kff.org/insurance/7049.cfm [accessed March 2007]).

45. *The Economist* (2004), "Headaches for All" October 9: 22–23.

46. Kerry (2004), "Plan to Keep High-Paying Jobs in America" (Washington, DC; available online at www.washtech.org/news/legislative/display.php?ID_Content=4740 [accessed March 2007]), October.

47. Although the events of September 11, 2001, created a sense of national crisis, this situation favored Republicans instead of Democrats.

48. Quadagno, *One Nation, Uninsured*.

49. For a general discussion about these issues, see Tom Sorell, ed. (1998), *Health Care, Ethics and Insurance* (London: Routledge).

50. Jonathan Weisman and Michael Abramowitz (2006), "Katrina's Damage Lingers For Bush: Many See Storm as President's Undoing," *Washington Post*, August 26: A01.

51. George W. Bush (2005), *President Discusses Hurricane Relief in Address to the Nation*, New Orleans (available online at www.whitehouse.gov/news/releases/2005/09/20050915-8.html [accessed March 2007]), September 15.

Conclusion

This book formulated two main sets of claims about state protection and the politics of insecurity.

First, state protection has become increasingly complex and multifaceted, and globalization can complicate the protective missions of the state and even increase the sense of collective insecurity. Still, globalization has not yet favored a strong decline of state power. At least in advanced industrial societies, massive income tax breaks and national actors propagating neoliberal ideas probably constitute a more direct menace to state protection than does economic globalization.

Undeniably, even in the United States, the era of "big government" is far from over. A long-term historical perspective shows how much the modern state has expanded over the past century. In the United States, by the 1910s:

> government expenditures per capita were about $129, or slightly more than four times the 1792 level. In 2004, the federal government spent $7,100 per capita, nearly 55 times more than was spent per capita in the 1910s. Spending growth did slow down in the mid-1980s and actually decrease in the mid-1990s. By the year 2000, however, per capita spending increased once again.[1]

A look at the number of cabinet departments confirms this long-term trend, which is common to most advanced industrial countries. In the United States, eight cabinet departments "were created from 1788 to 1952. Since 1953, there have been an additional eight cabinet departments established."[2] The two most recent federal departments created in the United States involve key components of state protection: the Environmental Protection Agency (1990) and Homeland Security (2002). The relatively recent creation of these two departments points to growing concerns about environmental and terrorist threats. From a historical perspective, "big government" is not getting smaller and is probably here to stay. This is especially true for issues of state protection.

Second, political leaders and other officials can play a major role in the construction of collective threats against which the state is meant to shield its citizens. The manner in which these actors frame the perceived threats of the day is tied to electoral strategies, social inequalities, and vested interests related to existing policies and market forces. The roles of the mass media and other civil social actors are sometimes crucial to the construction of collective insecurity.

Part II provided evidence for five basic claims on the central role of political leaders in this process. First, the comparative analysis stressed the limitations of the concept of moral panic, which applies only to a limited range of insecurity episodes. Second, this analysis confirmed the growing risk awareness of citizens even beyond environmental issues, and discussed the idea that people often blame politicians for problems for which they are not directly responsible, partly because citizens rely so much on the state for protection. Third, in part because they are exposed to so much potential criticism, political leaders attempt to deflect blame for bad news, and conversely claim credit for good news. Fourth, in framing their strategies, political leaders face powerful interests and institutional forces that create major constraints and opportunities for them. If we add the weight of the threat infrastructure—i.e., the general characteristics of the menace specific to a policy area—the capacity of political leaders to shape the perception of and to exploit collective insecurity faces major constraints. In other words, political leaders must take into account vested interests and the nature of the threat at hand when dealing with collective insecurity. Finally, the strategies of these actors can take the form of proactive or reactive behavior: political leaders can either help push a threat onto the agenda (proactive) or simply attempt to alter perception of this threat after other actors have transformed it into a major political issue (reactive).

These remarks clarify the argument about the political shaping of insecurity. Moreover, the four case studies provided evidence that the study of collective insecurity must recognize that political leaders and strategies carry much weight in the construction of collective insecurity. Yet, recognizing the central role of political leaders in the shaping of threats and even the propagation of fear should not hide that the state does protect citizens from genuine threats that can have dramatic consequences on the life of citizens. We should not forget that most threats that enter the policy arena have a foundation in reality.

One lesson of this book is that state protection and the politics of insecurity involve major tradeoffs that citizens and policymakers must keep in mind when they seek to fight older and newer threats. First, state protection involves potential tradeoffs between personal freedom and individual rights and lasting protection needs. There is no broad consensus about how far the state should go to protect national security and fight other collective threats ranging from environmental degradation to flight crashes to economic insecurity. In the United States, the contemporary debate over the Patriot Act illustrates the tension between personal freedom and the need for bolder state protection. Second, state protection and the politics of insecurity concern the allocation of scarce fiscal resources among a growing number of policy areas. Like the freedom-protection tradeoff, the allocation of fiscal resources is an inherently political issue that can trigger bold interest group mobilization. From airline companies to labor unions representing police officers, many collective actors fight over state protection priorities and the fiscal resources allocated to them. To this mobilization over concrete policy issues we can add the broad debate over the general need for tax cuts or tax hikes, a divisive issue that is related to class inequality.

The expansion of state protection can become a very controversial issue, especially when, in the absence of a shared sense of crisis, new protection measures involve possible tax increases or significant infringements upon personal freedom. Debates on these issues are rooted in profound fiscal and moral dilemmas. Such debates are also political, as the discourse of political leaders and the mobilization of interest groups greatly affect them.

Three Limitations

To stimulate future debate about state protection and the politics of insecurity, it is relevant to stress three limitations of this book. First, it does not offer definite answers about state protection and the politics of insecurity. More sociological studies are needed to improve the understanding of the threat infrastructure and the other factors and processes discussed above. Second, this book leaves to others the difficult task of determining whether collective insecurity is more present today than it was in the past.[3] In spite of sensationalist media coverage and growing risk awareness, there is no strong evidence that the general level of collective insecurity that people experience today is significantly higher than in the past, as the expansion of state protection may offset the increase in risk awareness. Nonetheless, in spite of higher life expectancy and a general increase in wealth and state protection, collective insecurity is still a crucial aspect of human life in advanced industrial societies; and, despite its lasting oppressive side, the national state still does protect citizens against major economic, environmental, and security threats. Future social science research could compare the transformation of the politics of insecurity at different historical stages in order to assess if the sense of collective insecurity is stronger or weaker today than in societies of the past.

Third, this book offers only limited insight into the relationship between public opinion and the political construction of insecurity. Considering this, we should not assume that the public is always easily manipulated and that the capacity of political leaders to construct collective insecurity and even manipulate the public is unlimited. As suggested in Chapter Five, citizens may become skeptical about what political leaders and other officials tell them are the "real threats." In the United States, growing popular disillusionment with the bloody war in Iraq and with the Bush Administration after the 2005 Katrina disaster show how popular skepticism has real political consequences. In this case, such skepticism contributed to the poor performance of the Republican Party at the 2006 midterm elections, which allowed Democrats to take control of both chambers of Congress for the first time since 1994. In the absence of new terrorist attacks on American soil, the terror alerts and apocalyptic discourse on the War on Terror that helped President Bush and his allies gain public support in the aftermath of September 11, 2001, became increasingly ineffective as ideological attacks from opponents and controversial policies like the Iraq War weakened their credibility and their capacity to deflect blame. In general, although the total lack of trust in state officials is rarely a positive thing, limited trust is probably better for democracy than blind obedience or the belief that political leaders have only the public interest in mind when dealing with collective insecurity and state protection.

Final Thoughts

This book does not aim to tell readers what they should or should not be afraid of. What it shows is how political leaders, in conjunction with media outlets and other actors, can inflate or downplay threats, or turn the public's attention toward specific sources of insecurity at the expense of others. Some contemporary fears may be blown out of proportion—for example, BSE does not kill as many people every year as the flu, a disease about which most citizens are far less concerned. However, greater risk awareness is not necessarily bad, as it increases the vigilance expected from ordinary citizens. Still, these citizens must keep in mind that, although related to genuine threats, many forms of collective insecurity are subject to political manipulation.

Because elected officials frequently have a perceived strategic interest in downplaying or dramatizing threats, calling for responsible political discourse about collective insecurity is probably naive. Yet informed citizens can take a more lucid look at state protection and the politics of insecurity. This more reasoned public understanding should be rooted in the assumption, implicit in Charles Tilly's state-making theory, that the state is both a genuine source of security and a potential oppressor. On one hand, the national state protects citizens against an increasing number of uncertainties, and it can effectively reduce collective insecurity. On the other, political leaders can use collective insecurity to justify attacks against domestic and foreign scapegoats, or to justify the enactment of measures that reduce the rights and freedoms of citizens without necessarily making them safer. For example, it is difficult to argue that the 2003 invasion of Iraq made the United States a much safer place than before; in fact, this invasion may have increased the dangers Americans face both at home and abroad.[4] The debate over this issue is part of the ongoing politics of insecurity in the United States and around the world.

Academics and informed citizens need to know more about the political construction of collective insecurity and the policy alternatives available to protect society more effectively against major collective threats. Today it is undeniable that the state is still crucial to our well being and that, as the example of the American healthcare system shows, private protection can aggravate the unequal distribution of risks and protection in advanced industrial societies. But recognizing the lasting and often positive role of the state in reducing collective insecurity should not justify isolationism and militant nationalism. Cooperation between national states and the construction of a supranational order that supplements national states instead of replacing them entirely may be innovative responses to global threats that these states cannot always fight alone.[5] This is true because stressing only the importance of emerging forms of global governance at the expense of traditional state protection may have negative consequences. Efforts to build integrated forms of governance should not lead citizens and activists to consider that the national state has no sustainable future.

Unfortunately, the post–September 11 focus on policing and national security may unduly narrow the meaning of state protection. Here, the idea that state protection has become increasingly complex and multifaceted could contribute to one of the most pressing issues of our time: the debate over the role of the national state in advanced industrial societies. Specific forms of social and environmental protection are under attack, and the post–September 11 obsession with terrorism and national security could impoverish the meaning of state protection and facilitate cutbacks and privatizations in other policy areas that could, in the long run, increase major forms of inequality and collective insecurity.[6] We should remember that the concept of collective insecurity refers not only to politically manipulated threats but also to a concrete lack of protection. In spite of political manipulation and repression, national states still offer *real* protection against genuine, yet socially constructed, threats.

Notes

1. Thomas A. Garrett and Russell M. Rhine (2006), "On the Size and Growth of Government," *Federal Reserve Bank of St. Louis Review*, January/February: 13–30.
2. Ibid., p. 14.
3. According to some theorists, contemporary societies exhibit greater levels of fear and insecurity than those of the past. See Frank Furedi (2002), *The Culture of Fear: Risk Taking and the Morality of Low Expectation* (London, Continuum International), and Andrew Tudor (2003), "A (Macro) Sociology of Fear?" *Sociological Review* 51(2): 218–37.
4. For a discussion about this issue, see Christopher Dickey and John Barry (2006), "Has the War Made Us Safer?" *Newsweek*, April 12 (available online at www.msnbc.msn.com/id/4661300/ [accessed March 2007]).
5. This form of cooperation should be grounded in the idea of interdependence. On this idea, see Benjamin R. Barber (2003), *Fear's Empire: War, Terrorism, and Democracy* (New York: W. W. Norton).
6. On the potential problems caused by the post–September 11 narrowing of state protection debates, see Robert Castel (2003), *L'insécurité sociale: Qu'est-ce qu'être protégé?* (Paris: La République des idées/Le Seuil).

Index